Healthy
Cookbook
for Two

Healthy Cookbook for Two
Quick Start Guide

PAGE 57

Need a healthy weeknight meal for two that you can quickly pull together after work? Try the Tomato Basil Pizza.

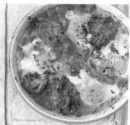

PAGE 124

Looking for something to cook for a leisurely Sunday brunch with your loved one? Make the Eggs Poached in Curry Sauce.

PAGE 201

Craving a simple two-person dessert? The Apple Cranberry Crumble is a satisfying follow-up to any meal that won't leave you feeling guilty.

Healthy Cookbook for Two

175 SIMPLE, DELICIOUS RECIPES TO ENJOY COOKING FOR TWO

ROCKRIDGE
PRESS

CONTENTS

The Meal You Share Together Is an Act of Love

W ho eats with you at night? Is it someone you plan to spend the rest of your life with? Is it your child, your parent, or another member of your family? You probably see this person every day. They know when you're happy, and they sense when you've had it rough. The person who eats with you at night is usually someone you care about. Maybe it's the person you love most in the world. The meal you share together is an act of love.

Cooking for two people isn't always easy. You're short on time, for one thing. Proportions for two people can be hard to measure, since most cookbooks are designed for big groups. You end up with strange amounts of leftovers—too much of one thing, not enough of something else. On top of that, you want to eat healthy. This is someone you care about, after all. Unhealthy food just won't do. The meals you share should nourish you both and keep you healthy for a long, long time. You want delicious recipes that cook quickly and fill you with good nutrients.

Healthy Cookbook for Two gives you plenty of fast, healthy, delicious meals that are perfect for a duo.

The trick to producing these fabulous meals with fresh, whole foods is having a strategy. You don't always want to eat leftovers, but a ready-made meal can be a relief when you need to grab and go. Cooking for two people requires smaller quantities of ingredients. Having leftover ingredients often means you need another recipe to use up the other half of your onion or can of beans so it doesn't molder under plastic wrap in the back of your refrigerator. A well-thought-out meal plan for the week allows you to use ingredients in more than one recipe. Creating a meal plan with your partner can also be a wonderful way to bond and discover new tastes to try. This book outlines how to do this planning and provides a comprehensive shopping list for a sample weekly meal plan (page 13) designed for two people without wasted or missing products. Dashing to the store for an absent ingredient cuts into the time you can spend enjoying your meals together, so shopping smart is the best strategy.

Chapter 2 is all about taking those fresh ingredients and using healthy cooking techniques to create wonderful meals. You can ruin your long-term health if you combine nutritious food with too much salt, fat, sugar, and preservatives. How you cook is as important as what you cook when you have an eye on your health. You will also learn about tricks developed by professional chefs to save time and effort when preparing meals. Learning to accurately double your recipes for company is also important, because some of your favorite recipes might not taste the same or turn out exactly as planned unless adjusted correctly. Handy make-ahead preparation tips as well as methods to use and store leftovers can leave you more time to take a walk together or snuggle on the couch.

The second part of *Healthy Cookbook for Two* is where you'll find over 175 healthy, scrumptious recipes that are simple to prepare and combine well together for an easy-to-execute weekly plan. You'll discover both weekday and weekend options that use everyday ingredients and cooking methods. Each recipe also provides nutritional data so you can see the calorie count and know how much fat, carbohydrates, and protein you are eating in each dish.

Healthy, home-cooked meals have never been easier to plan, create, and enjoy with the person you love. Use this cookbook as your guide, and most of all, have fun.

HEALTHY PAIRS

Committing to a healthy lifestyle is all about choices and making quality, nutritious food part of your daily routine. You might face a dilemma when it comes to food because you want to eat nutritious home-cooked dishes, but don't want to spend all your precious time shopping and preparing meals.

That is where planning and healthy cooking techniques come into play. Spending 30 minutes creating a meal plan every week can save you hours running around and sweating over a stove. Knowing how to prepare recipe components ahead, which ingredients cross over into more than one recipe, and fast, healthy cooking methods will make your meal creation fun and stress-free. Also, understanding how to get the most out of the groceries you buy can put money back in your pocket and reduce the graveyard of half-used ingredients in your refrigerator and pantry.

Healthy Cookbook for Two will help you set up a planning, shopping, and cooking approach that provides nutritious, enjoyable meals to nourish your body and spirit. This strategy is a sustainable solution that supports a lifetime of happy, healthy meals spent in the company of loved ones and friends.

Plan Ahead

The benefits of planning meals in advance

If there is a time- and money-saving tactic for creating healthy meals, it is *never go to the grocery store without a meal plan and a list*. Grocery stores are designed to entice you to spend more money and buy more than you need. So spend some valuable time planning your meals to avoid grocery pitfalls. There are many benefits to planning meals. Here are just a few.

➤   **Organizing your weekly meals can save money.** You can plan your meals so that ingredients overlap and you can double up on products. You can then buy larger quantities of some items and still have no waste at the end of the week. Planning also means a comprehensive grocery list with no dithering about in the store getting items you don't need. Buying everything at one time prevents emergency trips to the store and spending extra money on gas.

➤   **A well-thought-out weekly meal plan is like depositing precious time in the bank.** If you know what you will be making, prep ingredients earlier in the week, and have all the ingredients at home, you will save time. That extra time can be spent taking a walk, playing with a pet, or devoting quality time to a loved one. Planning your meals will also allow you to schedule quick dishes on busy days, and recipes that take more effort or time on evenings that aren't hectic. This strategy will reduce stress, creating a calmer atmosphere at home and improving your health.

➤   **A well-executed meal plan eliminates the temptation to eat out.** You won't be staring forlornly into a poorly stocked refrigerator agonizing over what to make for dinner. Eating at home saves money; it is also much healthier to create meals at home because you can source quality ingredients (who knows where most restaurants get their supplies?), while controlling your intake of fat, sugar, and salt.

> **Knowing your meals in advance allows you to double-prep ingredients.** For example, if you're making a soup on Wednesday that calls for sliced carrots and planning a shepherd's pie for Thursday that also requires sliced carrots, then you can slice both quantities at the same time. Use one batch for your soup and store the other half for the next day.

After a little practice, you will find that it is not hard to come up with a workable blueprint so your week runs smoothly. There are a few determining factors to consider each week as you develop your meal plan, such as:

> **Which days have evening activities?** These are your salad, slow cooker, and stir-fry days so you can eat something nutritious and dash out the door.

> **Do you have a nice variety of recipes?** When you are cooking for just two people, one of the issues is leftovers. If you are not careful, you might end up with a massive batch of chili and spend three days trying to finish it. This will not happen with *Healthy Cookbook for Two,* because the recipes are designed for only two people. So pick an assortment of recipes that feature chicken, lamb, vegetables, fish, beef, and nutritious grains.

> **Can some ingredients be prepped ahead, and how long will those prepared components last in the refrigerator?** Plan your most perishable meals, such as fish or seafood dishes, early in the week and save meals that use hearty ingredients, such as vegetarian chili, for later.

> **Is there an overlap of ingredients?** Craft a meal plan that has crossover in the ingredients while maintaining variety so you don't have to purchase a unique set of foods per meal. Look at the vegetables, starches, and proteins to see which recipes are similar but still unique enough to please your sense of culinary adventure. Here's an example:

SAMPLE WEEKLY MEAL PLAN

DAY	MEAL
Monday	Cod with Pesto Vegetables in Parchment
Tuesday	Arugula, Chickpea, and Cherry Tomato Salad
Wednesday	Sweet Potato Cakes
Thursday	Fresh Country Vegetable Soup
Friday	Jerked Pork Tenderloin with Mango Relish
Saturday	Sesame Vegetable Stir-Fry
Sunday	Chicken Broccoli Casserole

Using ingredients across multiple meals

It can be hard to judge the amount of ingredients needed for a week's worth of meals, especially when you are cooking for just two people. It is almost impossible to find certain ingredients in smaller amounts, such as a half-cup of tomato paste, or find an onion small enough to fill a quarter-cup when chopped. This can lead to food waste or an assortment of containers in the refrigerator. However, the accumulation of excess ingredients does not have to be a problem if you employ a practice used in professional kitchens around the world. Chefs are often paid bonuses for keeping their food costs down, so they design menus to use overlapping ingredients. This saves money and labor, and is an efficient method to cut down on waste.

You can use the same approach when planning your weekly meals and grocery shopping. Scan through the recipes first to see if certain ingredients show up in more than one recipe before choosing your weekly plan. Write your shopping list—including the required amounts—starting with the first recipe, and then go through each recipe on your meal plan. When you come across an ingredient that is already on the list, add the amount to the previous amount. By the end of all the recipes, you can see the required amount of each ingredient, and you will know which items can be purchased and prepped in bulk. Here's an example, based on the Sample Weekly Meal Plan above:

SHOPPING LIST FOR SAMPLE WEEKLY MEAL PLAN

INGREDIENTS	AMOUNT	DAY
MEAT (POULTRY, PORK, AND FISH)		
Chicken breasts	1 breast	7
Cod fillets	12 ounces	1
Pork tenderloin	10 ounces	5
DAIRY AND EGGS		
Egg	1	3
Butter	1 teaspoon	7
Parmesan cheese	¼ cup	7
PRODUCE		
Arugula	2 cups	2
Broccoli	1 head	4,6,7
Button mushrooms	6	6
Carrot	3	1,4,6
Celery	2 stalks	4,6
Cherry tomatoes	10	2
Cilantro	1 tablespoon	5
Cucumber	1	5
Garlic	3 fresh cloves (or from 1 jar)	3,4,5
Ginger	2-inch knob	6
Green beans	15 beans	4
Lime	1 lime	3,5
Mango	1	5
Red bell pepper	3	1,4,5,6
Scallion	1 bunch	2,5
Sweet onion	1	3,4,5
Sweet potato	1	3
Tomatoes	2	4
Zucchini	2	1,6
FROZEN		
Frozen whole-kernel corn	½ cup (from 1 bag)	4

INGREDIENTS	AMOUNT	DAY
GROCERY		
Bread crumbs	6 tablespoons	3,7
Chicken stock	8 ounces	1,7
Pesto	1 tablespoon	1
Sesame seeds	1 tablespoon	6
Sodium-free canned chickpeas	1 (16-ounce) can	2,3
Vegetable stock	3 cups	4
PANTRY ITEMS (STOCKED IN YOUR CUPBOARD)		
Balsamic vinegar	1 teaspoon (from 1 bottle)	2
Brown sugar	1½ teaspoons (from 1 bag)	5
Cayenne pepper	Dash	5
Dijon mustard	¼ teaspoon (from 1 jar)	2
Flour	1 teaspoon (from 1 bag)	7
Freshly ground black pepper	2 tablespoons	1,2,3,5
Ground allspice	Dash	5
Ground cinnamon	Dash	5
Ground nutmeg	½ teaspoon	7
Honey	1 tablespoon (from 1 jar)	6
Nonstick cooking spray	1 bottle	1
Olive oil	¼ cup + 2 teaspoons (from 1 bottle)	2,3,4,5
Red wine vinegar	1 tablespoon (from 1 bottle)	5
Sea salt	¼ teaspoon	2,3
Sesame oil	1 teaspoon (from 1 bottle)	6
Tamari sauce	¼ cup (from 1 jar)	5,6
Uncooked brown rice	1½ cups	7

10 tips for buying for two people and making the groceries last

A growing trend in grocery shopping is products sold in big-box stores in huge quantities. Unfortunately, these gigantic boxes of canned tomatoes and bags of apples are not the best choice when cooking for two people. More often than not, you end up with piles of unused food in your pantry or food in the garbage. Shopping for two people is not difficult, but there are definitely tricks you can employ to limit your food waste and save money. Here are the top ten:

1. Find a quality butcher and fishmonger so you can pick the smaller portion sizes you need for your recipes.

2. Look for bags of frozen peeled and deveined shrimp that can be resealed, so you can take out what you need and put the bag back in the freezer.

3. If you're buying fresh, avoid big bags of fruits and vegetables; instead, hand-pick loose produce so you reduce the chance you will end up throwing unused, spoiled items out.

4. Buy puréed herbs in handy squeeze tubes instead of bunches—they keep longer in the refrigerator. Or if you want to use fresh herbs, purée the excess and freeze the purée in ice cube trays.

5. Look for packages of greens, precut vegetables, and containers of prepared fruit that match the amounts you need in your recipes.

6. Buy nonperishables in larger quantities. Utilize sealed storage bins for bulk dry items, like rice, flour, and sugar. If you have freezer space, it can also be extremely economical to get frozen fruits and vegetables in large, resealable bags.

7. Buy in season and locally when you can. Seasonal fruit tastes better and can be significantly less expensive than produce shipped across the country.

8. If you can't get smaller amounts of an ingredient such as tomato sauce or chicken stock, use what you need and freeze the remaining product in ice cube trays for other recipes.

9. Shop the bulk section and salad bars. The bulk section is a source of many products that you might need in smaller quantities, such as nuts, dried fruits, and bread crumbs. The salad bar is where you can pick and choose certain ingredients such as cherry tomatoes or olives.

10. Have a list. The best strategy for shopping for two people is to plan your week and have a list.

Cook Healthy

Healthy cooking techniques

The cooking techniques you use to create your meals can be as important as the food you eat. What is the point of buying nutritious, unprocessed ingredients and then deep-frying them or boiling them until all the nutrients are leached out? Luckily, the simplest and most commonly used cooking techniques are the healthiest. These methods retain the flavor and unique characteristics of your ingredients, creating scrumptious meals. Here are healthy ways to cook:

➤ **Baking:** Baking does not add fat or extra calories to the finished product and is effective for meat dishes, sides, and casseroles.

➤ **Blanching:** This cooking method is quick but requires supervision to create perfect results. Blanching is when you briefly submerge vegetables, fruits, meats, and seafood in boiling water.

➤ **Braising:** This cooking technique uses both dry and moist heat to create a tender product in a rich sauce. The only fat comes from the oil used to brown the meat or poultry before the entire pot is covered and placed in the oven to finish in an enclosed moist-heat environment.

➤ **Broiling:** Broiling is a bit like backward grilling: You place your food under a high-heat source *in* the oven rather than *over* it, as with grilling. Broiling should be done on a rack placed over a pan so that the fat from the food drips into the pan below.

➤ **Grilling:** Grilling is a versatile cooking technique that is appropriate for almost any ingredient, including fruit. Grilling adds smoky flavor and allows the fat in the food to drip down and away.

- ➤ **Poaching:** Poaching is an extremely gentle fat-free method of cooking that submerges the ingredients in gently simmering liquid. This technique creates a tender finished product infused with the flavor of the poaching liquid, such as stock, wine, juices, or just herb-laced water.

- ➤ **Roasting:** Roasting is done at higher temperatures, usually over 400°F, in the oven. Roasting is superb for meats, poultry, and vegetables.

- ➤ **Sautéing:** This can be a healthy cooking method for small pieces of food if you don't use a lot of oil or fat. Water, stock, and wine are all great substitutions if you don't need to brown the ingredients.

- ➤ **Steaming:** Cooking with steam is easy and quick, and adds no fat or extra calories. Simply place your ingredients in a perforated pan or dedicated steamer over simmering water (which can be infused with herbs or wine), or a dedicated steamer. The food retains much of its nutritional content, and in some situations, the leftover pan liquid can be used to make stock.

- ➤ **Stir-frying:** This is a quick, traditional Asian cooking style done with a little healthy oil, water, or stock. Ingredients are cut into small pieces and tossed in a nonstick pan over high heat.

Make-ahead meals

Have you ever wondered how professional chefs seem to put out dozens, if not hundreds of meals effortlessly when it is often difficult for home cooks to do one? The secret to this culinary "magic" is found in the hours of unseen work that happen before the first guest sits down in the dining room. Professional chefs have containers, bottles, and bowls of ingredients arranged on their well-organized station. This collection of ingredients is called *mise en place*, meaning "to put in place." So it is not magic, just good planning, which you can also do at home to make your cooking stress-free.

Your own weekly *mise en place* does not have to be as ruthlessly complete as a chef's, but there are components you can have prepared to speed up the cooking process. Keep in mind that some preparation cannot be done ahead of time, and ingredients cannot keep indefinitely in the refrigerator. Make sure you label the contents of each container with the date and recipe. Here are some *mise en place* ideas to simplify your cooking life for the recipes in this book:

➤ Bake or grill any chicken breasts, steaks, or fish needed for salads, wraps, sandwiches, and cooking with steam is easy and quick, and adds no fat or extra calories. Simply place your ingredients in a perforated pan or dedicated steamer over simmering water (which can be infused with herbs or wine), or a dedicated steamer. The food retains much of its nutritional content, and in some situations, the leftover pan liquid can be used to make stock.

➤ Cut up vegetables and refrigerate each type in different sealed containers for up to five days. For example, if you need diced carrots in two recipes, you can store both quantities in one sealed container.

➤ Cook the rice or grains you need for salads and casseroles, and refrigerate them in sealed containers for up to four days.

➤ Cook beans or legumes and refrigerate them in sealed containers for up to five days.

➤ Hard-boil—but do not peel—eggs for salads, curries, sandwiches, and casseroles, and refrigerate them for up to one week.

➤ Mix together salad dressings and refrigerate them in sealed containers for up to two weeks.

➤ Blend any spice or dried herb mixture, and store in sealed baggies or containers in a cool dark place for up to one month.

Doubling recipes

The recipes in *Healthy Cookbook for Two* are designed to create portions for two people, so you don't have unused ingredients taking up space and growing crops of mold in your refrigerator. These smaller-yield recipes also limit the amount of leftovers you produce as well. But what if you want leftovers or guests are coming for dinner and you need to double your favorite *Healthy Cookbook for Two* recipe? Do you just multiply everything by two, or is there a recipe-doubling strategy? Doubling a recipe is simple, but there are some important guidelines to ensure success, which are:

➤ Make sure you write down the original recipe and then put the doubled recipe amounts right beside each ingredient, so you don't forget anything.

➤ Never double baking recipes. Baking is a science, and each percentage of baking soda, flour, and liquids is calculated to produce an effect. If you need double quantities, make two single recipes.

- In nonbaking recipes, you can double all the main ingredients: meats, poultry, fish, vegetables, fruits, grains, legumes, eggs, dairy, flour, and sweeteners. So, for example, you would use two apples instead of one, or 1 cup of rice instead of ½ cup.

- Use bigger pots or baking dishes for the doubled version to keep the same cooking time and temperature. For example, if the original recipe uses a 6-by-6-by-3-inch baking dish, make sure you use a 9-by-9-by-3-inch for the larger recipe (the depth of the food in the pan should be the same). It is smart to monitor the dish until it is completed.

- Use 1½ times the seasonings (spices, herbs, salt, hot sauces) from the original amount, and adjust the seasoning if you want more impact. So if the original recipe calls for 2 teaspoons of basil, the doubled recipe should need 1 tablespoon.

- Do not double the oil or fat used to sauté or brown the ingredients. Use enough to lightly coat the bottom of the skillet or pan.

Using leftovers

- Sometimes there is food to spare after a lovely meal, so it is important to know the safest way to store and reuse your leftovers.

- Place your leftovers in the refrigerator in a shallow, uncovered container as soon as they cool to room temperature and stop steaming. This will prevent any bacteria growth that might shorten the shelf life of the food.

- After the food is cool, cover the container with a tight-fitting lid so the food doesn't dry out in the refrigerator, and eat within two to three days.

- Keep different types of leftovers in separate containers.

- If you don't think you are going to eat your leftovers within a couple of days, it is best to freeze them. Place them in individual containers, and when they are completely chilled, cover the container tightly. Label all the containers with the date and contents before freezing.

- If your leftovers are frozen, thaw them in the refrigerator overnight.

- Always reheat your leftovers to a minimum temperature of 165°F.

- Eat your leftovers immediately after they are thawed; do not continue a "leftover cycle" by saving your remaining leftovers.

You can also create delicious meals from leftover cooked components such as steaks, chicken breasts, fish fillets, vegetables, and rice. Some interesting uses for these ingredients are:

➤ Meats can be used for salads, sandwiches, or tasty casseroles.

➤ Poultry is wonderful for casseroles, soups, sandwiches, salads, creamy chicken or turkey salad, and frittatas.

➤ Fish is delicious in salads, sandwiches, soups, and casseroles.

➤ Cooked vegetables have many uses. Potatoes can be cubed and sautéed for home fries, as well as stirred into casseroles, soups, and stews. Mashed potatoes can be stirred into soups to thicken them. Grilled vegetables are delicious chopped into pasta sauces or arranged as a salad.

➤ Cooked rice and grains are a wonderful base for casseroles, stirred into soups, or featured in cold salads.

10 tips to eat healthy for life

➤ **Simplify your food expectations:** Healthy eating is a long-term commitment to yourself, so the plan you put in place to achieve this goal needs to be sustainable. You certainly don't want to be measuring, weighing, and chronicling your food intake for the rest of your life, so toss out those expectations. Look for fresh, wholesome ingredients, eat a range of colors every day, and find simple-to-prepare recipes.

➤ **Fruits and vegetables should be your diet base:** The majority of your plate should be made up of a broad range of colorful, nutrient-packed produce. Fruits and vegetables are low in calories and fat, so it is difficult to overeat and gain weight when you make them the majority of the meal.

➤ **Eat healthy fat**: Fat is not the enemy. You need healthy fats for almost every system in the body. Assuming you are a healthy weight, you should eat between 25 and 30 percent healthy fats per day. Healthy fats are monounsaturated fats (almonds, olive oil, seeds) and polyunsaturated fats, which include omega-3 and omega-6 (walnuts, flaxseed oil, fatty fish such as salmon). You should also eliminate or reduce saturated fats from your diet (mostly from animal sources) and trans fats (found in processed foods).

➤ **Include protein in your diet:** Protein contains the building blocks of the body in the form of 20 amino acids. The body can make most of these amino acids, but there are nine that only come from the food you eat. That means getting protein is important, but it should only represent about 30 percent of your diet. Quality sources of protein include lean poultry, lean meat, fish, eggs, beans, nuts, seeds, and soy products.

➤ **Watch your portion sizes:** Healthy food can still cause weight gain when you eat too much of a good thing. You might have to weigh your meats, fish, and seafood initially so you get a good idea of what 5 or 6 ounces looks like on your plate. With a little practice you should be able to eyeball a healthy portion size.

➤ **Eat vegetarian meals half the time:** You don't have to convert to a complete vegetarian lifestyle, but research is piling up that indicates a vegetable-based diet can improve general health and add years to your life. Fruits and vegetables are packed with disease-fighting antioxidants. Eating a diet high in the saturated fat found in meat and dairy products can increase our risk of cardiovascular disease, Alzheimer's, and cancer. So ditch the meat and poultry at least three times a week.

➤ **Limit sugar and salt:** If you are eating wholesome, unprocessed foods, your sugar and salt intake should be minimal anyway unless you add these ingredients yourself. Sugar causes a slew of health concerns and is linked to obesity, diabetes, cardiovascular disease, cancer, and autoimmune diseases. Salt is often overused, and this excess can lead to hypertension and cardiovascular disease. The body does need between ½ and 1 teaspoon of sodium per day, so use sea salt sparingly and watch added salt in the food you eat.

➤ **Plan to succeed:** Meal planning is critical to maintaining a healthy diet because if you know what you are eating and have the ingredients on hand and the time to cook, it is unlikely you will pick up fat- and sodium-laden fast food or takeout.

➤ **Read nutrition labels:** Whole-grain pasta, lentils, and tomatoes are packaged products that you will probably buy for convenience. It should be second nature to scan the nutrition label on ingredients for hidden sugar, saturated fat, and sodium.

➤ **Eat with company and no distractions**: One of the true pleasures of eating is to share the meal with a person you love. This type of intimate, casual interaction is crucial after a stressful day. Eating together means talking, looking into each other's eyes, and leaving the electronics away from the table. Mindful eating without the distraction of TV or other devices means you pay attention to your food and are less likely to overeat.

SHOPPING FOR TWO:
Handy foods to have on hand for this cookbook

REFRIGERATOR ITEMS

- Butter
- Cheeses: low-fat Cheddar, low-fat or fat-free cottage cheese, goat cheese, reduced-fat or fat-free mozzarella, Parmesan
- Eggs
- Garlic, minced
- Ginger, minced or whole root
- Herbs, fresh
- Nut and soy milks
- Skim milk
- Sour cream, fat-free
- Yogurt, low-fat or fat-free plain and vanilla

NUTS, SEEDS, AND OILS

- Coconut, unsweetened, shredded
- Flaxseed
- Nut and seed butters, natural
- Nuts (almonds, cashews, hazelnuts, pecans, and more), unsalted and roasted
- Olive oil
- Seeds (flaxseed, sesame, and sunflower; pine nuts)
- Sesame oil

GRAINS AND LEGUMES

- Barley
- Beans (black beans, chickpeas, Great Northern beans, kidney beans, lentils, pinto beans), dried or sodium-free canned
- Quinoa
- Rice, brown or wild
- Whole-grain breads, pitas, tortillas
- Whole-wheat bread crumbs

PANTRY GOODS

- Baking powder
- Black pepper/peppercorns
- Brown sugar
- Cocoa powder, unsweetened
- Coconut milk, light canned
- Dijon mustard
- Dried fruit (apricots, cranberries, dates, raisins)
- Flours (whole-wheat, all-purpose)
- Honey
- Hot sauce
- Maple syrup, pure
- Oatmeal
- Olives
- Rice noodles
- Salsa
- Sea salt
- Soba noodles

- Spices (allspice, cinnamon, whole cloves, coriander, cumin, curry, nutmeg, and more)
- Stock (beef, chicken, and vegetable) low-sodium, nonfat
- Tahini
- Tamari sauce, low-sodium
- Tomatoes, sodium-free canned
- Tomato paste, low-sodium
- Tomato sauce
- Vanilla extract, pure
- Vinegar (apple cider, balsamic, red wine, rice)
- Whole-grain pasta

WEEKNIGHT RECIPES

Weeknights can be hectic, and the last thing you might want to do when you get home from work is cook. However, one of the most important strategies for living a full, healthy life is home cooking, because you can control what you are serving. Wholesome natural ingredients and healthy cooking methods combine to create balanced dishes that nourish the body. Sharing meals prepared with attention and care with a loved one can be the best way to end a busy day. Putting nutritious, delicious food on the table in a reasonable time frame is not difficult; it just takes planning and an easy-to-follow recipe.

These weekday choices range from crisp, refreshing salads that can be thrown together in minutes to rich hearty stews that allow you to handle a few chores while the stew cooks in the oven. You will discover something to suit every palate, arranged in easy-to-navigate sections such as Soups and Stews, Fish and Seafood, and Vegetarian Entrées. There are recipes for every evening schedule and energy level. What the dishes have in common are healthy ingredients, easy execution, and that they are designed to be enjoyed by two people. You might find so many tempting meal ideas that these recipes will not just be for weeknights anymore.

Salads

PREP TIME
10 MINUTES

Greens and Snow Peas Salad

This colorful salad has very few ingredients but packs a powerful taste punch. Peppery arugula, ripe raspberries, and fresh, crisp snow peas are splashed with a bit of sweet, pungent balsamic vinegar. Although these ingredients are available year-round in most places, raspberries are in season in early summer. The best raspberries are picked fragrant and warm from the sun and sold in local farmers' markets.

1. Arrange the greens evenly on two serving plates. Arrange the snow peas and scallion on the greens. Scatter the fresh raspberries on the tops of the salads. Drizzle with balsamic vinegar and season with freshly ground black pepper.

2. Serve immediately or store in the refrigerator, covered, without the vinegar. Drizzle the vinegar over the salad right before serving.

TIP: *Sugar snap peas can replace the snow peas, especially if you have some fresh from the garden. You may need to remove the strings from either kind if the pods are mature.*

PAIR WITH . . . Fruit Tarts (page 199)

2 cups baby spinach

1 cup arugula

½ cup snow peas, trimmed and halved

1 scallion, white and green parts, cut into ⅛-inch slices

1 cup raspberries

1 tablespoon good-quality balsamic vinegar

Freshly ground black pepper

PER SERVING
Calories: 62
Fat: 0.7g
Saturated fat: 0.0g
Protein: 3.3g
Carbohydrates: 12.2 g
Sodium: 30mg
Fiber: 6.1g
Sugar: 4.9g

Creamy Cucumber Salad

GLUTEN-FREE
MAKE AHEAD
30 MINUTES

PREP TIME
10 MINUTES

Is this a salad, sauce, dip, or spread? This is a trick question because this cool, rich concoction can be all of these dishes. You might want to double or triple the recipe so you always have this salad on hand. Cucumber bursts with juice and tastes like a fresh spring morning. It's a fantastic ingredient for a make-ahead salad. This proliferation of juice is the reason you need to squeeze the excess liquid out of the shredded cucumber. Adding salt to cut or shredded cucumber makes the liquid drain faster, but you can omit the salting step if you have any issues with hypertension. You can also omit the salt if you are saving the cucumber juice to use in a refreshing drink or smoothie. This salad is best made with fresh mint.

2 English cucumbers

¼ teaspoon sea salt

1 scallion, white and green parts, cut into ⅛-inch slices

½ cup fat-free plain Greek yogurt

2 tablespoons chopped fresh mint, or 1 tablespoon dried mint

1 tablespoon freshly squeezed lime juice

1 tablespoon honey

¼ teaspoon finely grated lime zest

2 tablespoons pine nuts

PER SERVING
Calories: 217
Fat: 6.5g
Saturated fat: 0.0g
Protein: 15.4g
Carbohydrates: 28.2g
Sodium: 345mg
Fiber: 2.8g
Sugar: 13.4g

1. Slice the cucumbers very thinly and place them in a fine mesh sieve. Sprinkle the slices with the salt and set the sieve over a bowl and let sit for about 15 minutes so the moisture can drain .

2. Press the cucumbers to remove as much liquid as possible and transfer them to a medium bowl. Add the scallion and stir to combine.

3. In a small bowl, whisk together the remaining ingredients except the pine nuts until well blended.

4. Add the dressing to the cucumbers and stir to mix well. Serve topped with pine nuts.

TIP: *If you have any extra salad, this recipe makes a perfect topping for lamb burgers. It also tastes even better after sitting for a day in the refrigerator, so double the recipe. If more liquid seeps out of the cucumber while the salad chills, just pour it out before dressing the salad.*

PAIR WITH . . . Apple Cranberry Crumble (page 201)

PREP TIME
15 MINUTES
(+ chilling time)

COOK TIME
35 MINUTES

Beet, Watermelon, and Radish Salad

The elements of this salad are especially vibrant because of all the different shades of red. The burgundy hue of beets, the bright red of the watermelon, and the scarlet of the radishes next to their snowy white centers is simply glorious. Small, seedless watermelons are now widely available, and are perfect for this salad, since a personal-size melon is the exact amount needed. To save time, prep the rest of the ingredients while you roast the beets.

1. Preheat the oven to 350°F.

2. Place the beets on a baking sheet and drizzle them with the olive oil. Roast until the beets are tender, about 35 minutes. Cool the beets.

3. Transfer the beets to a large bowl. Add the remaining ingredients and toss well. Refrigerate, covered, for at least 30 minutes.

TIP: *Purchasing watermelon can be tricky because you never know what you are getting until you cut the melon open. To get a juicy, sweet melon, look for one that has a dark-green rind, feels heavier than it should for its size, and has a yellow (not white or pale-green) spot on one side—called a "field spot"—where the watermelon rested on the ground as it ripened.*

PAIR WITH . . . Nutmeg-Baked Peaches (page 199)

5 medium beets, peeled and cut into 1-inch chunks
1 teaspoon olive oil
1 small (4- to 5-pound) seedless watermelon, rind cut off and cut into 1-inch chunks
3 radishes, quartered
½ cup shredded spinach
2 tablespoons chopped parsley, or 1 tablespoon dried parsley
Juice of 1 lemon

PER SERVING
Calories: 158
Fat: 2.6g
Saturated fat: 0.0g
Protein: 3.4g
Carbohydrates: 40.1g
Sodium: 116mg
Fiber: 4.8g
Sugar: 35.1g

Green Papaya Salad

GLUTEN-FREE
DAIRY-FREE
MAKE AHEAD
30 MINUTES

PREP TIME
20 MINUTES
(+ soaking and
chilling time)

Green papaya has a firm, almost vegetable taste that combines beautifully with spicy sauces and is very popular in Asian fusion cooking. In this recipe you are basically substituting an unripe fruit for the cabbage in a traditional slaw. You will know immediately if the papaya is too ripe for this recipe when you start to run it over the grater. Green papaya is sold in produce sections of Asian markets. Select a firm one, with no blotchy areas or soft spots, and store it in a plastic produce bag in the refrigerator.

2 green papayas, peeled, seeded, and shredded or julienned

1 grapefruit, peel and pith removed, sliced

1 scallion, white and green parts, cut into ⅛-inch slices

¼ English cucumber, diced

1 green bell pepper, seeded, deribbed, and julienned

Juice of 1 lime

1 tablespoon peanut butter

1 teaspoon minced garlic

1 teaspoon low-sodium tamari sauce

1 teaspoon brown sugar

Pinch red pepper flakes

1 tablespoon chopped fresh basil

1. Put the shredded papaya in a bowl of cold water and soak for 2 hours. Drain and transfer to a large bowl. Add the grapefruit, scallion, cucumber, and bell pepper. Toss to combine.

2. In a small bowl, stir together the lime juice, peanut butter, garlic, tamari, brown sugar, and red pepper flakes until well blended. Add the dressing to the salad along with the cilantro and mix well.

3. Refrigerate the salad for at least 1 hour to let the flavors meld.

TIP: *Use a vegetable peeler to remove the papaya skin with very little waste of the luscious flesh. You can also try unripe mangos in this recipe if papaya is unavailable in your supermarket.*

PAIR WITH . . . Chocolate Oat Bites (page 201)

PER SERVING
Calories: 205
Fat: 4.2g
Saturated fat: 0.9g
Protein: 5.8g
Carbohydrates: 38.2g
Sodium: 401mg
Fiber: 6.7g
Sugar: 22.4g

Arugula, Chickpeas, and Cherry Tomato Salad

Salad is a versatile part of a healthy diet, so you might like having a go-to vinaigrette to use for many different combinations of ingredients. The simple Dijon dressing in this recipe is a classic and can be made in larger quantities so you have it on hand for all your greens. Store your dressing in a pretty glass jar in the refrigerator, and jazz it up with fresh herbs such as thyme, basil, or chives.

1. In a large bowl, whisk together the olive oil, vinegar, and mustard. Season with salt and pepper. Add the arugula and toss to dress the greens.

2. Arrange the greens on two serving plates, evenly divide the chickpeas, cherry tomatoes, and scallion between the plates, and serve.

TIP: *Refrigerate the remaining chickpeas in a plastic sealed container. Use them in hummus or curries, or roast them in the oven with a little spice for a tasty snack.*

PAIR WITH . . . Mixed Berries with Orange Cream (page 198)

1 teaspoon olive oil

1 teaspoon good-quality balsamic vinegar

¼ teaspoon Dijon mustard

Sea salt

Freshly ground black pepper

2 cups arugula

1 cup sodium-free canned chickpeas, rinsed and drained

10 cherry tomatoes, halved

1 scallion, white and green parts, cut into ⅛-inch-thick slices

PER SERVING
Calories: 182
Fat: 4.3g
Saturated fat: 0.6g
Protein: 9.3g
Carbohydrates: 31.9g
Sodium: 165mg
Fiber: 10.5g
Sugar: 16.8g

Roasted Carrot and Cherry Tomato Salad

GLUTEN-FREE
DAIRY-FREE
MAKE AHEAD

This hearty salad could be a starring dish at a fall harvest festival. The sweet, earthy taste and fragrance of roasted carrots are comforting on a chilly autumn day. This salad is delicious served alongside a spice-rubbed grilled pork tenderloin. Use packaged baby carrots if you don't have time to cut up whole carrots into matchsticks. The easiest way to create even carrot sticks (or other sliced vegetables) is with a mandoline. This handy kitchen device can be a huge time-saver if you prepare a great deal of produce.

PREP TIME
15 MINUTES

COOK TIME
25 MINUTES

4 large carrots (about 1 pound), peeled and cut into 3-inch matchsticks

1 cup cherry tomatoes, halved

½ red onion, cut into eighths

2 tablespoons prepared basil pesto

2 tablespoons chopped cashews or pecans

2 tablespoons chopped fresh parsley, or 1 tablespoon dried parsley

PER SERVING
Calories: 234
Fat: 12.9g
Saturated fat: 1.0g
Protein: 4.7g
Carbohydrates: 35.7g
Sodium: 241mg
Fiber: 9.3g
Sugar: 14.0g

1. Preheat the oven to 450°F.

2. In a medium bowl, toss the carrots, tomatoes, and onion with the pesto until well coated.

3. Transfer the vegetables to a baking sheet and roast until the carrots are tender, about 25 minutes. Remove from the oven and let cool for 10 minutes.

4. Transfer the vegetables to a serving bowl and top with the nuts and parsley. Serve warm or chilled.

TIP: *Dried herbs are more concentrated than fresh ones, so you need less of them. Often, the ratio is 1 to 3; however, this book uses a slightly different ratio. Start with the recommended amounts and adjust to your taste. Remember, you can always add more, but you can't take it away. Buy bulk dried herbs, found in co-ops and most well-stocked supermarkets, for the best taste.*

PAIR WITH . . . Tropical Fruit Salad with Creamy Lime Sauce (page 198)

Shaved Asparagus Salad with Almonds

If you need a culinary offering to tote along for a family event or neighborhood potluck, this dazzling dish is the perfect choice. The ingredients are common items at your local grocery store, but the method of presenting them is unique and fun. Peeling the asparagus into ribbons creates striking light and dark green strips that pair exquisitely with the creamy white and yellow of the chopped eggs. This salad is best in early spring when asparagus is in season, tender and fresh.

1. In a small bowl, whisk together the olive oil, vinegar, and garlic, and season with salt and pepper. Set aside.

2. Use a peeler to make thin asparagus ribbons, and transfer them to a large bowl. Add the eggs, almonds, and dressing to the asparagus and toss to combine. Serve topped with the Asiago.

TIP: *Try to find asparagus spears just slightly wider than a pencil so that peeling them is easier.*

PAIR WITH . . . Pecan Honey Bananas (page 200)

1 tablespoon olive oil

1 teaspoon good-quality balsamic vinegar

½ teaspoon minced garlic

Sea salt

Freshly ground black pepper

20 asparagus stalks (about ½ pound), trimmed of the woody ends

2 hard-boiled eggs, peeled and grated

1 tablespoon chopped almonds

2 tablespoons grated Asiago cheese

PER SERVING
Calories: 225
Fat: 17.4g
Saturated fat: 2.7g
Protein: 14.1g
Carbohydrates: 5.7g
Sodium: 190mg
Fiber: 2.8g
Sugar: 2.7g

Roasted Asparagus and Tomato Pasta Salad

GLUTEN-FREE
MAKE AHEAD
30 MINUTES

PREP TIME
15 MINUTES
COOK TIME
5 MINUTES

Do you have a balcony or patio at home where you enjoy intimate lunches and dinner alfresco? You might want to include this Greek-inspired salad and a chilled glass of white wine for those special meals. Creamy goat cheese replaces the more traditional feta in this salad for a less salty bite. Goat cheese is so rich and luscious that you might be surprised to find out it has fewer calories and fat than most other cheeses: only 70 calories and 6 grams of fat in 1 ounce. So include this nutrient-packed cheese in your healthy diet in moderation without guilt.

1 tablespoon olive oil, divided

1 tablespoon freshly squeezed lemon juice

1 teaspoon honey

1 teaspoon grainy mustard

1 teaspoon chopped fresh basil, or ½ teaspoon dried basil

¼ teaspoon freshly ground black pepper

6 asparagus spears, trimmed of the woody ends and cut into 2-inch pieces

12 cherry tomatoes, halved

2 cups cooked penne pasta

¼ cup pitted Kalamata olives, sliced

1 cup baby spinach

1 ounce goat cheese, crumbled

1. Preheat the oven to 400°F.

2. In a small bowl, whisk together 2 teaspoons of olive oil, lemon juice, honey, mustard, basil, and pepper, and set aside.

3. Toss the asparagus and tomatoes with the remaining 1 teaspoon of olive oil and roast in the oven for 5 minutes. Remove from the oven and set aside for 15 minutes to cool in a large bowl.

4. Add the pasta, olives, spinach, and dressing and toss to combine. Serve topped with the cheese.

TIP: *This is a full-meal salad that can be enjoyed on a balmy summer evening. Include a thick slice of crusty French bread to round out the meal.*

PAIR WITH . . . Speedy Strawberry Ice Cream (page 198)

PER SERVING
Calories: 440
Fat: 14.1g
Saturated fat: 4.8g
Protein: 15.0g
Carbohydrates: 60.2g
Sodium: 232mg
Fiber: 5.3g
Sugar: 6.8g

PREP TIME
15 MINUTES

COOK TIME
10 MINUTES

Chinese Sesame Noodle Salad

Noodles are an integral component in Chinese cuisine. There are many tasty types of noodles, so this recipe does not specify which you should use. Lo mein and udon noodles are superb in this dish because they soak up the piquant sauce. If you have a gluten sensitivity, then rice vermicelli is an acceptable option. You might want to throw together this salad for a picnic lunch in the park—it is fabulous cold and can be put together the day before.

1. Cook the noodles according to package directions with no added salt or oil. Drain and set aside in a large bowl.

2. In a small bowl, whisk together the sesame oil, vinegar, tamari sauce, garlic, and chili paste.

3. To the noodles, add the dressing, broccoli, carrot, bell pepper, snow peas, and scallion and toss to combine. Serve topped with the sesame seeds.

TIP: *This salad is even better the second day after the noodles and vegetables have had time to soak up the flavorful dressing. Try adding shredded chicken for a more substantial meal.*

PAIR WITH . . . Gingered Melon (page 198)

½ (4-ounce) package
  uncooked Chinese noodles

1 tablespoon sesame oil

1 tablespoon rice vinegar

1 teaspoon low-sodium
  tamari sauce

½ teaspoon minced garlic

¼ teaspoon chili paste

1 cup small broccoli florets

1 carrot, peeled and cut into
  ⅛-inch-thick matchsticks

1 red bell pepper, seeded,
  deribbed, and cut into
  ⅛-inch-thick strips

½ cup halved snow peas

1 scallion, white and green
  parts, diagonally cut into
  ⅛-inch-thick slices

1 tablespoon sesame seeds

PER SERVING
Calories: 459
Fat: 26.8g
Saturated fat: 3.8g
Protein: 10.1g
Carbohydrates: 46.0g
Sodium: 641mg
Fiber: 6.9g
Sugar: 6.0g

Couscous Avocado Salad

A staple ingredient in North African cooking, couscous has gained popularity in other areas of the world, especially France, Italy, and the UK. Many people think these tiny grains are just that—a grain. But couscous is closer to a pasta and is made from durum wheat. It is light and fluffy when prepared correctly, and you can make the instant varieties in about ten minutes. If you want a more flavorful base for this salad, keep in mind that couscous becomes infused with the flavor of whatever liquid you cook it in, so try chicken stock, apple juice, or even tea.

2 tablespoons olive oil

1 tablespoon apple cider vinegar

1 teaspoon chopped fresh oregano, or ½ teaspoon dried oregano

Sea salt

Freshly ground black pepper

1 cup cooked couscous

1 celery stalk, diced

10 cherry tomatoes, halved

¼ English cucumber, diced

½ avocado, diced

2 tablespoons crumbled feta cheese

1 tablespoon chopped fresh parsley, or 1 teaspoon dried parsley

1. In a small bowl whisk together the olive oil, vinegar, and oregano. Season with salt and pepper and set aside.

2. In a large bowl, toss together the remaining ingredients until well mixed. Add the dressing and toss to combine.

3. Refrigerate for 1 hour and serve.

TIP: *The leftover avocado can be stored in the refrigerator for a few days if sprinkled with lemon juice and wrapped tightly in plastic. It can be used up in smoothies, sandwiches, or dips, and as a thickener for puddings and brownies.*

PAIR WITH . . . Citrus Curd with Berries (page 199)

PER SERVING
Calories: 456
Fat: 27.3g
Saturated fat: 5.7g
Protein: 11.1g
Carbohydrates: 49.0g
Sodium: 268mg
Fiber: 12.5g
Sugar: 16.9g

Soups and Stews

PREP TIME
10 MINUTES

COOK TIME
15 MINUTES

Green Vegetable Soup with Pesto

Green foods always seem to imply vibrant health and wellness. This soup is packed with green goodness, featuring several bright- and dark-hued vegetables that simply burst with nutrients. Green herbs and vegetables usually sport this color because they contain a great deal of chlorophyll, which is a complex chemical involved in photosynthesis. Chlorophyll is a healthy addition to your diet because it is a powerful blood cleanser; it also boosts the blood's ability to carry oxygen, creating a hostile environment for bacteria growth. Eat lots of this green vegetable soup to promote a healthy immune system and increase longevity.

1. Heat the olive oil in a medium stockpot over medium-high heat. Sauté the leek, celery, and garlic until softened, about 2 minutes.

2. Add the chicken stock and bring to a simmer. Reduce the heat to low, and add the green beans and peas. Simmer until the vegetables are tender, about 5 minutes. Add the spinach and thyme; simmer 1 minute more.

3. Remove the pot from the heat and stir in the lemon juice, lemon zest, and pepper. Serve immediately, topped with the pesto.

TIP: *Pesto is a staple item that can be utilized in countless recipes and as a flavor boost for stews, sauces, and marinades. You can also mix it into mayonnaise to create a tasty spread for any sandwich. Look for prepared pesto with minimal salt or make your own.*

PAIR WITH . . . Citrus Curd with Berries (page 199)

1 tablespoon olive oil
1 leek, white and light-green parts sliced and washed thoroughly
1 celery stalk, diced
1 teaspoon minced garlic
3 cups sodium-free chicken stock
½ cup green beans, trimmed and cut into 1-inch pieces
½ cup fresh or frozen green peas
1 cup shredded spinach
1 tablespoon chopped fresh thyme or 1 teaspoon dried thyme
Juice of ½ lemon
1 teaspoon lemon zest
¼ teaspoon freshly ground black pepper
1 tablespoon prepared or homemade basil pesto

PER SERVING
Calories: 161
Fat: 8.6g
Saturated fat: 1.1g
Protein: 6.9g
Carbohydrates: 19.1g
Sodium: 237mg
Fiber: 4.5g
Sugar: 4.5g

Fresh Country Vegetable Soup

GLUTEN-FREE
DAIRY-FREE
ONE-POT

PREP TIME
10 MINUTES

COOK TIME
25 MINUTES

Planning to make this soup can be as fun as the actual preparation because any fresh vegetable can be thrown in the pot with delicious results. This flexibility means a morning spent strolling through a farmers' market can provide inspiration for the recipe. Look for the freshest produce possible, and use your senses to pick the right choices. Inhale the earthy scent of fresh-pulled carrots and parsnips; gently cup ripe, warm tomatoes to see if they are firm and bruise-free; and break a few green beans to hear and see their juicy snap. There are few things more enjoyable and satisfying than selecting quality ingredients to create a special meal.

1 teaspoon olive oil

½ sweet onion, chopped

½ teaspoon minced garlic

1 celery stalk, diced

½ red bell pepper, seeded, deribbed, and diced

3 cups low-sodium vegetable stock

2 tomatoes, diced

½ cup sliced carrots

½ cup green beans, trimmed and cut into 1-inch pieces

½ cup small broccoli florets

½ cup frozen whole-kernel corn

1 teaspoon hot pepper sauce

PER SERVING
Calories: 149
Fat: 3.1g
Saturated fat: 0.0g
Protein: 4.8g
Carbohydrates: 28.2g
Sodium: 252mg
Fiber: 6.6g
Sugar: 10.1g

1. Heat the olive oil in a medium stockpot over medium-high heat. Sauté the onion, garlic, celery, and bell pepper until softened, about 4 minutes.

2. Add the vegetable stock, tomatoes, carrots, and green beans to the pot. Bring the soup to a boil; then reduce the heat to low. Simmer the soup until the vegetables are crisp-tender, about 15 minutes. Add the broccoli and corn, and continue to simmer for 3 minutes.

3. Remove the pot from the heat and stir in the hot sauce. Serve immediately.

TIP: *This soup is even better with fresh corn kernels, so whenever possible, pick up a golden ripe ear to add to the other fresh ingredients. Simply stand the ear up in a bowl and use a sharp knife to slice the kernels off close to the cob. The bowl will catch the kernels.*

PAIR WITH . . . Multigrain Chips (page 182)

PREP TIME
10 MINUTES

COOK TIME
30 MINUTES

Fiery Chickpea Soup

If you are a fan of Southwest black bean soups, this light soup might become a new favorite. Chickpeas, also known as garbanzo beans, are a staple food in many parts of the world and are valued for their fiber and nutrient content. They are marvelous for stabilizing blood sugar, creating a feeling of fullness, and can cut the risk of cancer. It is a smart idea to keep cans of sodium-free chickpeas as a pantry item because they can be used in soups, stews, dips, salads, and even in desserts. Drain and rinse canned beans thoroughly.

1. Heat the olive oil in a medium stockpot over medium-high heat. Sauté the onion and garlic until softened, about 2 minutes.

2. Add the chicken stock, chickpeas, carrot, tomato, and chile; bring to a boil. Reduce the heat to low and simmer until the vegetables are tender, about 20 minutes.

3. Purée soup in a blender until smooth and add the lemon juice. Season with salt and pepper. Serve topped with the yogurt.

TIP: *The seeds in chile peppers are where most of the heat comes from, so if you want a milder soup, remove the seeds and ribs from the chile. Wash your hands thoroughly after dicing chiles because the juice can cause severe irritation to your eyes.*

PAIR WITH . . . Pecan Honey Bananas (page 200)

1 teaspoon olive oil

1 cup chopped sweet onion

2 teaspoons minced garlic

3 cups low-sodium
chicken stock

1 (15-ounce) can chickpeas,
rinsed and drained

1 carrot, peeled and diced

1 ripe tomato, diced

½ fresh chile (such as serrano
or jalapeño), diced

Juice of ½ lemon

Sea salt

Freshly ground black pepper

1 tablespoon fat-free
plain yogurt

PER SERVING
Calories: 341
Fat: 5.6g
Saturated fat: 0.8g
Protein: 21.7g
Carbohydrates: 50.4g
Sodium: 279mg
Fiber: 16.3g
Sugar: 8.3g

Tuscan White Bean Soup with Kale

Tuscan food is a cuisine that fits firmly in the healthy Mediterranean diet group. This cooking features olive oil, spinach, beans, garlic, tomatoes, and lots of herbs. This hearty soup has all those elements, with shredded kale replacing spinach. Kale is a superstar ingredient that is easily available in any grocery store. If you are more familiar with spinach, keep in mind that kale has a stiffer texture that requires more time to wilt in the hot soup.

PREP TIME
10 MINUTES

COOK TIME
20 MINUTES

1 teaspoon olive oil

½ sweet onion, peeled and chopped

2 teaspoons minced garlic

1 celery stalk, diced

3 cups sodium-free vegetable stock

1 tomato, diced

1 (15-ounce) can sodium-free Great Northern beans, rinsed and drained

1 carrot, peeled and diced

2 cups stemmed and chopped kale

1 tablespoon chopped fresh basil, or 1 teaspoon dried basil

¼ teaspoon red pepper flakes

Sea salt

Freshly ground black pepper

2 tablespoons grated Parmesan cheese

1. Heat the olive oil in a medium stockpot over medium-high heat. Sauté the onion, garlic, and celery until softened, about 5 minutes.

2. Add the vegetable stock, tomatoes, beans, and carrot. Bring the soup to a boil; then reduce the heat to low. Simmer the soup until the carrot is tender, about 10 minutes. Add the kale, basil, and red pepper flakes, and simmer for an additional 2 minutes.

3. Season with salt and pepper. Serve topped with the Parmesan.

TIP: *Great Northern beans are the perfect ingredient for soups because they hold their shape even after prolonged boiling. They also have an interesting melt-in-your-mouth texture and mild taste that combines well with other ingredients.*

PAIR WITH . . . Cheese-Stuffed Pears (page 200)

PER SERVING
Calories: 412
Fat: 10.3g
Saturated fat: 4.4g
Protein: 22.0g
Carbohydrates: 59.3g
Sodium: 611mg
Fiber: 18.6g
Sugar: 8.4g

Classic Minestrone

Minestrone is a big, hearty soup—which is appropriate because according to some culinary historians, the word *minestrone* means "big soup." Recipes for minestrone vary, with most versions including tomatoes, beans, and seasonal vegetables. Minestrone was thought to be a vegetarian soup originally, mostly due to the scarcity of meat long ago, but some modern recipes include chunks of beef or lamb. This version is a filling meal rather than an appetizer. You could easily make it completely vegetarian by using vegetable stock instead of chicken stock.

PREP TIME
20 MINUTES

COOK TIME
20 MINUTES

1. Heat the olive oil in a medium stockpot over medium-high heat. Sauté the onion, garlic, celery, and fennel until softened, about 3 minutes.

2. Add the stock, tomatoes, zucchini, and beans to the pot, stirring to mix. Bring to a boil; then reduce the heat to low. Simmer the soup for 15 minutes to combine the flavors; then stir in the spinach.

3. Season with pepper. Serve topped with the Parmesan.

TIP: *Fennel is a pale, graceful-looking vegetable with a distinct licorice taste that combines beautifully with tomato. Any leftover fennel can be grated and made into a fresh slaw combined with carrot, scallion, and julienned mango.*

PAIR WITH . . . Nutmeg-Baked Peaches (page 199)

1 teaspoon olive oil
½ sweet onion, peeled and chopped
1 teaspoon minced garlic
1 celery stalk, diced
¼ fennel bulb, shredded
1 cup sodium-free chicken stock
1 can (14.5 ounces) diced tomatoes
1 zucchini, cut into ½-inch chunks
½ can (7 ounces) kidney beans, rinsed and drained
½ cup spinach
Freshly ground black pepper
2 tablespoons grated Parmesan cheese

PER SERVING
Calories: 213
Fat: 9.2g
Saturated fat: 4.5g
Protein: 15.2g
Carbohydrates: 16.6g
Sodium: 367mg
Fiber: 5.4g
Sugar: 3.3g

Thai Seafood Soup

GLUTEN-FREE
DAIRY-FREE
30 MINUTES
ONE-POT

PREP TIME
15 MINUTES

COOK TIME
15 MINUTES

The seafood listed in the ingredients here are simply suggestions, so feel free to use any type you might have in your refrigerator. This recipe is a perfect choice for people who like to cook by the seat of their pants, throwing in a pinch of this or that on a whim. The heat-accented flavor of the stock combines well with any addition, but it can also be changed to suit your palate. It is also a wonderful soup to make as a team because its flexible nature lends itself to collaboration.

1 teaspoon sesame oil

1 teaspoon minced garlic

1 teaspoon peeled, minced fresh ginger

1 red bell pepper, seeded, deribbed, and julienned

2 cups sodium-free chicken stock

½ cup canned clam juice

4 sea scallops, halved

1 (6-ounce) haddock fillet, cut into 1-inch chunks

1 scallion, white and green parts, cut into ⅛-inch-thick slices

½ cup grated carrot

Zest of ½ lime

Juice of 1 lime

2 tablespoons chopped cilantro leaves

½ teaspoon reduced-sodium tamari sauce

¼ teaspoon red pepper flakes

1. Heat the sesame oil in a large stockpot over medium-high heat. Sauté the garlic and ginger until softened, about 3 minutes.

2. Add the chicken stock and clam juice, and bring to a boil. Reduce the heat to low, and add the scallops, haddock, scallion, bell pepper, and carrot. Simmer for 5 to 8 minutes, until the seafood is cooked.

3. Add the lime zest, lime juice, cilantro, tamari sauce, and red pepper flakes. Serve immediately.

TIP: *Any fish can be used for this soup, even leftover cooked fish or shrimp. Simply chop up the cooked fish or shrimp and add it at the end of the cooking time.*

PAIR WITH . . . Gingered Melon (page 198)

PER SERVING
Calories: 256
Fat: 18.8g
Saturated fat: 1.0g
Protein: 35.1g
Carbohydrates: 14.8g
Sodium: 708mg
Fiber: 2.2g
Sugar: 5.3g

PREP TIME
10 MINUTES

COOK TIME
35 MINUTES

Chicken Barley Soup

You might be more used to eating barley soups that partner beef instead of chicken with this nutritious grain. This recipe is a lighter version of those winter warming dishes, with lean chicken and swirls of shredded fresh spinach floating in the thyme-accented stock. The addition of ground chicken also cuts the cooking time considerably because you don't have to simmer the soup for hours to create tender beef chunks. So after a long day, you can be sitting down with your feet up and a tray of this soup on your lap in less than an hour. That leaves lots of time for a leisurely walk in the park after the dishes are done.

1. Heat the olive oil in a large saucepan over medium-high heat. Add the ground chicken and sauté until cooked through, about 5 minutes. Remove the chicken with a slotted spoon to a plate.

2. Add the onion, celery, and carrot to the saucepan and sauté until the vegetables are softened, about 3 minutes. Put the chicken back in the saucepan, along with the stock, barley, and thyme. Bring to a boil; then reduce the heat to low. Simmer the soup until the barley is tender, about 25 minutes.

3. Season with salt and pepper. Stir in the spinach and serve.

TIP: *If you don't want bunches of unused fresh herbs in your refrigerator, you can purchase handy tubes of puréed herbs and squeeze out what you need for each recipe. These prepared herb pastes keep much longer than bunches.*

PAIR WITH . . . Velvety Chocolate Pudding (page 202)

1 teaspoon olive oil
¼ pound lean ground chicken
½ sweet onion, chopped
1 celery stalk, chopped
1 carrot, peeled and cut crosswise into ¼-inch-thick slices
3 cups sodium-free chicken stock
¼ cup pearl barley
1 tablespoon chopped fresh thyme, or 1 teaspoon dried thyme
Sea salt
Freshly ground black pepper
1 cup baby spinach, shredded

PER SERVING
Calories: 266
Fat: 28.3g
Saturated fat: 2.2g
Protein: 22.5g
Carbohydrates: 26.0g
Sodium: 417mg
Fiber: 6.0g
Sugar: 3.1g

Turkey Noodle Soup

DAIRY-FREE
MAKE AHEAD
ONE-POT

PREP TIME
15 MINUTES

COOK TIME
25 MINUTES

You will be reminded of childhood when you enjoy a big bowl of this flavorful, noodle-packed soup. Noodle soups are a comforting choice of moms everywhere when their children are under the weather. Chicken soup can cure the common cold, it seems, so why can't this turkey-packed version also support good health? Turkey is high in protein and low in fat, which makes it a great choice for a diet focused on longevity. Turkey also contains tryptophan, an amino acid, which is linked to improving the immune system.

1 teaspoon olive oil

1 teaspoon minced garlic

½ sweet onion, chopped

1 carrot, peeled and diced

1 celery stalk, diced

3 ounces cooked turkey breast, diced into ½-inch chunks

3 cups sodium-free chicken stock

1 tablespoon chopped fresh thyme or 1 teaspoon dried thyme

½ cup baby spinach

2 ounces cooked whole-wheat noodles

Freshly ground black pepper

1. Heat the olive oil in a medium stockpot over medium-high heat. Sauté the garlic and onion until softened, about 3 minutes.

2. Add the carrot, celery, turkey, stock, and thyme. Bring to a boil; then reduce the heat to low.

3. Simmer the soup until the vegetables are tender, about 15 minutes.

4. Add the spinach and noodles and simmer until heated through, about 2 minutes more. Season with pepper and serve.

TIP: *This soup is a perfect way to use up leftover turkey from Thanksgiving or Christmas. The dark meat is equally good for soup. Feel free to experiment with the ingredients.*

PAIR WITH . . . Maple Pecan Tapioca Pudding (page 202)

PER SERVING
Calories: 214
Fat: 4.7g
Saturated fat: 1.0g
Protein: 15.2g
Carbohydrates: 27.4g
Sodium: 642mg
Fiber: 4.6g
Sugar: 5.2g

PREP TIME
15 MINUTES

COOK TIME
60 MINUTES

Irish Lamb Stew

Irish stew is true peasant food; it was traditionally made with tough cuts of meat and old root vegetables left over in the cellar after a long winter. Its light broth is perfect for soaking chunks of crusty (or even day-old) bread. As this soup tastes even better on the second or third day, prepare it over the weekend and reheat for an easy meal on hectic weeknights.

1. Heat the olive oil in a large saucepan over medium-high heat. Add the lamb chunks and cook them until browned on all sides, about 4 minutes. Using a slotted spoon, transfer the lamb to a plate.

2. Add the onion and garlic and sauté until softened, about 3 minutes. Return the lamb along with any juices on the plate to the pot. Add the stock and bring to a boil, then reduce the heat to low and simmer for about 35 minutes.

3. Add the celery, carrot, potato, and thyme. Simmer the stew, covered, for another 15 minutes, or until the lamb is tender. Season with salt and pepper and serve.

TIP: *Lamb stew was originally developed for cooking older, tougher cuts of mutton after the sheep were no longer good wool producers. The lamb available now is younger and more tender, so it is no longer necessary to braise it for hours and hours.*

PAIR WITH . . . Apple Cranberry Crumble (page 201)

1 teaspoon olive oil

2 (5-ounce) lamb chops, trimmed of fat and cut into 1-inch chunks

½ sweet onion, finely chopped

1 teaspoon minced garlic

2 cups sodium-free chicken stock

1 celery stalk, sliced

1 carrot, peeled and sliced

1 large potato, diced

1 tablespoon chopped fresh thyme, or 1 teaspoon dried thyme

Sea salt

Freshly ground black pepper

PER SERVING
Calories: 438
Fat: 12.0g
Saturated fat: 3.7g
Protein: 42.2g
Carbohydrates: 38.7g
Sodium: 363mg
Fiber: 5.9g
Sugar: 4.2g

Hearty Beef Barley Chili

MAKE AHEAD
ONE-POT

PREP TIME
15 MINUTES

COOK TIME
40 MINUTES

People plan entire weekends around chili festivals and contests because making good chili is an art. Some people like it so spicy that you can't taste anything for days, and others swear that it isn't real chili if you use ground beef instead of chunks of sirloin. This recipe is a mildly spicy version (with ground beef), but instead of beans, it calls for nutty barley. Barley is a pleasing choice for dishes that have lots of herbs or spices because it soaks up those flavors, creating another layer of complexity. Make sure you rinse the barley thoroughly in clean, cold water to remove any debris before adding it to your chili pot.

1 tablespoon olive oil
½ pound extra-lean
    ground beef
1 sweet onion, chopped
3 cups sodium-free beef stock
½ cup medium pearl barley
1 (28-ounce) can
    crushed tomatoes
1 green bell pepper, seeded,
    deribbed, and diced
1 teaspoon chili powder
½ teaspoon ground cumin
1 teaspoon fresh chopped
    oregano, or ½ teaspoon
    dried oregano
1 tablespoon fat-free
    sour cream

PER SERVING
Calories: 437
Fat: 9.8g
Saturated fat: 4.3g
Protein: 40.8g
Carbohydrates: 47.9g
Sodium: 337mg
Fiber: 8.4g
Sugar: 5.4g

1. In a 4–6 quart stockpot over medium-high heat, add the olive oil followed by the beef and onion. Cook, stirring, until the beef is cooked through and browned, 6 to 7 minutes. Carefully drain excessive fat if necessary.

2. Add the beef stock, barley, crushed tomato, bell pepper, chili powder, cumin, and oregano. Bring the chili to a boil; then reduce the heat to low.

3. Simmer the chili until the barley is tender and the liquid is almost completely absorbed, about 35 minutes. Serve topped with the sour cream.

TIP: *Barley has a nutty flavor and should have a slightly chewy texture even when cooked. This versatile grain helps promote digestive and cardiovascular health.*

PAIR WITH . . . Chunky Applesauce (page 201)

Vegetarian Entrées

Open-Faced Spinach and Fried Egg Sandwich

PREP TIME
10 MINUTES

COOK TIME
10 MINUTES

Eggs are one of the easiest ingredients to prepare for a meal. They are also a logical choice when you want something quick, homemade, and nutritious. Eggs have a little bit of a tarnished reputation as a contributor to high cholesterol and heart disease. If you are in good health with no underlying conditions, then having eggs a few times a week is beneficial. This healthy diet strategy includes the yolk because the yolk contains about 90 percent of the egg's iron and calcium. Eggs are a fabulous source of protein, which can be particularly important if you follow a vegetarian diet. So don't worry too much, and treat yourself to an egg dish for dinner every once in a while, as well as at breakfast. This yummy open-faced sandwich works well morning or night.

1. Preheat the oven to broil.

2. Lightly spray both sides of the bread with the cooking spray. Broil bread until lightly toasted, about 1 minute per side.

3. In a small bowl, toss the spinach and lemon juice together and set aside.

4. Heat the olive oil in a small skillet over medium-high heat, and fry the eggs until the whites are set, about 2 to 3 minutes.

5. Spread the cottage cheese on the toast and top with the dressed spinach. Slide one egg per sandwich onto the spinach. Season with pepper and sprinkle each egg with half of the Parmesan. Serve one open-faced sandwich per person.

TIP: *Spinach is one of the most nutritious foods in the world, containing almost 1,000 percent of the daily recommended amount (RDA) of vitamin K and 100 percent of the RDA of vitamin A. It is also very high in iron, manganese, and folate.*

PAIR WITH . . . Simple Roasted Baby Potatoes (page 191)

2 slices whole-wheat or
   multigrain bread
Nonstick cooking spray
1 cup spinach
1 teaspoon freshly squeezed
   lemon juice
1 teaspoon olive oil
2 eggs
¼ cup fat-free cottage cheese
Freshly ground black pepper
2 tablespoons grated
   Parmesan cheese

PER SERVING
Calories: 279
Fat: 15.0g
Saturated fat: 6.5g
Protein: 22.9g
Carbohydrates: 14.1g
Sodium: 557mg
Fiber: 2.1g
Sugar: 2.4g

Garden Veggie Crustless Quiche

GLUTEN-FREE
MAKE AHEAD
30 MINUTES

PREP TIME
5 MINUTES

COOK TIME
25 MINUTES

Quiche is often thought of as a French dish best served at a fancy luncheon. But quiche is actually German in origin and was originally a thrifty meal featuring common, inexpensive ingredients. The original recipes used bread to hold the tasty fillings, but eventually the bread evolved into flaky pastry. This recipe doesn't use a crust at all. The crust is often where most of the calories are found, so eliminating it creates a lower calorie and lower fat dish that can be enjoyed on a healthful diet.

3 eggs
2 egg whites
¼ cup skim milk
¼ cup shredded reduced-fat mozzarella cheese, divided
1 teaspoon butter, divided
3 button mushrooms, chopped
1 scallion, white and green parts, chopped
½ cup shredded spinach
6 cherry tomatoes, quartered
Freshly ground black pepper

PER SERVING
Calories: 249
Fat: 11.1g
Saturated fat: 4.4g
Protein: 21.4g
Carbohydrates: 18.9g
Sodium: 294mg
Fiber: 5.1g
Sugar: 12.5g

1. In a small bowl, beat the eggs, egg whites, milk, and half of the cheese until well blended; set aside.

2. Preheat the oven to 350°F. Grease 2 (8-ounce) ramekins with ¼ teaspoon of butter and set aside.

3. Melt the remaining ¾ teaspoon of butter in a small skillet. Sauté the mushrooms and scallion until softened, about 2 minutes. Add the spinach and sauté until wilted, about 1 minute.

4. Evenly divide the vegetables and the tomatoes between the ramekins. Pour in the egg mixture, dividing it evenly, and top each quiche equally with the remaining cheese. Bake until the quiches are puffed and lightly browned, about 15 to 20 minutes. Serve warm or cold seasoned with pepper.

TIP: *These mini quiches can be sliced up and used as the filling to a tasty toasted sandwich served in bed on a special morning. Add some fresh fruit to the plate.*

PAIR WITH . . . Sautéed Mixed Vegetables (page 190)

Portobello Mushroom Quesadillas

Quesadillas are an undeniably fun food best eaten with your hands. One can almost imagine a sunny patio with salt-kissed ocean breezes and icy margaritas when you bite into this crunchy meal. Quesadillas are often associated with South-western cuisine, but the meaty mushrooms and garlic-accented basil pesto in this recipe have a decidedly Mediterranean feel. If you can't find a good prepared pesto, you can also whip up your own in a blender with fresh basil, garlic, olive oil, Parmesan cheese, and pine nuts.

1. Heat the olive oil in a skillet over medium-high heat. Sauté the mushrooms until they are tender, about 4 minutes. Remove from the heat and set aside.

2. Preheat the grill to medium.

3. Spread 1 tablespoon of pesto on each of the tortillas. Divide the mushrooms, sun-dried tomatoes, and scallion evenly between the tortillas, spreading them out. Sprinkle each tortilla with 2 tablespoons of cheese. Fold the tortillas in half, pressing them gently to flatten.

4. Place the tortillas on the grill and cook for 2 minutes per side, until lightly grilled. Serve one quesadilla per person.

TIP: *For the best results, squeeze out any excess liquid from the cooked mushrooms, or they will make the tortillas soggy. If you don't have a grill, you can cook these quesadillas in a lightly oiled skillet over medium heat for about 2 minutes per side until the cheese melts.*

PAIR WITH . . . Grilled Asparagus (page 188)

1 teaspoon olive oil

2 medium portobello mushroom caps (about 3 inches in diameter), thinly sliced

2 (8-inch) whole-wheat tortillas

2 tablespoons prepared basil pesto

4 sun-dried tomatoes, chopped

1 scallion, white and green parts, cut into ⅛-inch-thick slices

¼ cup shredded low-fat Monterey Jack cheese

PER SERVING
Calories: 183
Fat: 9.8g
Saturated fat: 3.2g
Protein: 7.9g
Carbohydrates: 25.2g
Sodium: 257mg
Fiber: 3.6g
Sugar: 3.5g

Pinto Bean Falafel

MAKE AHEAD
30 MINUTES

PREP TIME
15 MINUTES

COOK TIME
10 MINUTES

This dish may be the most fun you've had in a long time. It is not just messy; it is downright sloppy, with dripping sauce, scattering toppings, and a great deal of dribbling juices on the chin. But it is well worth the mess because it is so delicious. Just have extra napkins handy, and enjoy yourself. This recipe uses creamy pinto beans instead of the more traditional chickpeas.

1 cup canned pinto beans, rinsed and drained

¼ cup shredded low-fat Cheddar cheese

2 tablespoons whole-wheat bread crumbs

1 tablespoon finely chopped scallion

¼ teaspoon ground cumin

Pinch ground coriander

1 egg white

1 teaspoon olive oil

1 (6-inch) pita, cut into two pockets

¼ avocado, diced

1 plum tomato, diced

2 tablespoons fat-free sour cream

Juice from ½ lime

PER SERVING
Calories: 303
Fat: 12.5g
Saturated fat: 4.4g
Protein: 14.8g
Carbohydrates: 36.5g
Sodium: 475mg
Fiber: 9.7g
Sugar: 2.0g

1. In a medium bowl, coarsely mash the beans with a fork. Add the cheese, bread crumbs, scallion, cumin, and coriander, and mix well. Stir in the egg white until thoroughly combined and the bean mixture holds together. Shape the bean mixture into two ½-inch thick patties.

2. Heat the olive oil in a large skillet over medium-high heat. Cook the patties until they are browned, turning once, about 3 minutes per side.

3. Stuff each pita half with one patty, and divide the avocado and tomato evenly between them.

4. Top each pita half with 1 tablespoon sour cream and a squeeze of lime juice. Serve one half per person.

TIP: *These patties can be served with Creamy Cucumber Salad (page 29) alongside as a main course without stuffing them into a pita. If you want a gluten-free option, purchase gluten-free pitas and replace the bread crumbs with almond meal, gluten-free oats, or crushed corn tortillas.*

PAIR WITH . . . Cinnamon Couscous (page 193)

Quinoa Chile-Stuffed Tomatoes

Tomatoes and other vegetables make handy, appetizing containers for a variety of fillings. The trick to great stuffed vegetables is finding those that are perfectly ripe, yet firm enough to hollow out. If a tomato is too ripe, it will sag, and if it is too green, you will have a hard time cutting through it. Tomatoes get more nutritious when cooked: baking them in the oven, as in this recipe, increases their levels of lycopene, a powerful disease-fighting antioxidant. Whenever possible, try to find orange varieties of tomatoes because their lycopene is easier for the body to absorb. Try growing your own tomatoes in the garden or in containers on your deck for the ultimate flavor and health experience.

1. Cut the tops off the tomatoes and discard. Carefully scoop out the insides of the tomatoes, taking care to leave the shell intact. Coarsely chop half of the tomato pulp, reserving the rest for another use. Sprinkle the inside of the shells with the salt, and turn the tomatoes upside down on paper towels for 30 minutes to drain the juices. After 30 minutes, turn the tomatoes hollow-side up and place them in a small baking dish.

2. Preheat the oven to 350°F.

3. Heat the olive oil in a large skillet over medium-high heat. Sauté the onion, garlic, and chile until softened, about 2 minutes. Add the corn and chopped tomato pulp. Cook for about 1 minute. Remove the skillet from the heat and add the remaining ingredients, mixing well.

4. Divide the vegetable-quinoa mixture evenly between the tomatoes. Bake for 20 minutes, until the filling is heated through and the tomatoes are softened. Serve hot.

TIP: *Use the remaining tomato pulp in sauces, salsas, soups, and stews. Store it in the refrigerator in a sealed container for up to 5 days, or freeze and use within a month.*

PAIR WITH . . . Tropical Fruit Salad with Creamy Lime Sauce (page 198)

2 large tomatoes
½ teaspoon sea salt
1 teaspoon olive oil
½ sweet onion, chopped
1 teaspoon minced garlic
½ chile (such as jalapeño or serrano) pepper, minced
½ cup fresh or frozen corn kernels
1 cup cooked quinoa
1 tablespoon chopped fresh cilantro
1 teaspoon freshly squeezed lime juice
½ teaspoon ground cumin
Pinch freshly ground black pepper
2 tablespoons grated Parmesan cheese

PER SERVING
Calories: 340
Fat: 11.5g
Saturated fat: 4.7g
Protein: 17.7g
Carbohydrates: 45.0g
Sodium: 741mg
Fiber: 6.7g
Sugar: 7.2g

Tomato Basil Pizza

MAKE AHEAD
30 MINUTES
ONE-POT

PREP TIME
10 MINUTES

COOK TIME
5 MINUTES

Pizza is often the ultimate casual indulgence, dripping with cheese and stacked high with cured meats. This vegetarian version is quite elegant-looking and light on the arteries. It is also an incredibly quick meal if you use a premade crust rather than kneading and rising your own dough. The crust used in this recipe is not a ball of dough, but rather something that looks like a huge pita bread. These crusts are often sold with a handy packet of prepared pizza sauce. But that sauce is often very high in sodium and sugar, so toss it in favor of healthier options, like the pesto used here.

1 (8-inch) prepared pizza crust

Nonstick cooking spray

2 tablespoons homemade or prepared basil pesto

1 tomato, thinly sliced

2 tablespoons chopped fresh basil or 1 tablespoon dried basil

Pinch red pepper flakes

¼ cup shredded reduced-fat mozzarella cheese

PER SERVING
Calories: 144
Fat: 5.1g
Saturated fat: 1.3g
Protein: 7.1g
Carbohydrates: 24.5g
Sodium: 407mg
Fiber: 1.0g
Sugar: 2.8g

1. Place a rack in the middle of the oven and preheat the oven to broil.

2. Place the crust on a baking sheet and lightly spray the edges with the cooking spray. Spread the pesto on the crust so that it covers the whole surface except for a ½-inch border around the edges. Arrange the tomato slices on the pizza in overlapping concentric circles. Sprinkle the basil and red pepper flakes evenly over the tomatoes. Sprinkle the cheese evenly over the basil.

3. Place the pizza in the oven and broil until the crust is crispy and the cheese is melted, about 5 minutes. Cut the pizza into 4 slices and serve 2 slices per person.

TIP: *The entire pizza can be made ahead and refrigerated until you want to eat it. You can also use a favorite pizza crust recipe for this recipe, and simply adjust the cooking time to compensate for using raw dough. If you do use raw dough (also available premade at many markets), make sure to stretch it as thin as possible on the baking sheet for an authentic crunchy crust.*

PAIR WITH . . . Speedy Strawberry Ice Cream (page 198)

PREP TIME
5 MINUTES

COOK TIME
20 MINUTES

Lemon Asparagus Linguine

In many households, making a simple pasta dinner entails opening a jar or can of prepared tomato sauce and heating it on the stove to eventually pour over some noodles. The misconception about other kinds of pasta dishes is that anything outside of canned sauce takes a long time to prepare. But in fact, some of the most flavorsome recipes take less than 30 minutes from cutting board to stove and onto your plate. This citrusy dish is a great example of a homemade meal you can make quickly after work. If you want to save time and skip a step, blanch the asparagus ahead of time and refrigerate it in a sealed container until you cook the sauce.

1. Blanch the asparagus until crisp-tender in boiling water, about 2 minutes. Quickly cool the asparagus under cold running water. Set aside.

2. Heat the olive oil in a large skillet over medium-high heat. Sauté the garlic until softened, about 2 minutes. Add the flour and whisk to create a paste, about 1 minute. Whisk in the milk, thyme, lemon juice, and zest. Reduce the heat to medium and cook the sauce, whisking constantly, until thickened and creamy, about 3 minutes. Stir in the linguine, asparagus, and 2 tablespoons of the Parmesan.

3. Transfer to two plates and top each plate with 1 tablespoon of the remaining Parmesan.

TIP: *Lemon creates a clear, fresh taste in this pasta sauce that combines perfectly with tender asparagus. Lemons are a wonderful source of vitamin C and great for detoxing the body.*

PAIR WITH . . . Cheese-Stuffed Pears (page 200)

16 asparagus spears, trimmed of woody ends and cut into 2-inch pieces

1 teaspoon olive oil

2 teaspoons minced garlic

2 teaspoons all-purpose flour

1 cup skim milk

1 tablespoon chopped fresh thyme or 1 teaspoon dried thyme

1 tablespoon freshly squeezed lemon juice

½ teaspoon lemon zest

2 cups cooked whole-wheat linguine

¼ cup grated Parmesan cheese, divided

PER SERVING
Calories: 403
Fat: 11.1g
Saturated fat: 5.3g
Protein: 28.2g
Carbohydrates: 50.7g
Sodium: 531mg
Fiber: 9.2g
Sugar: 10.6g

Squash Macaroni and Cheese

This recipe is a sneaky way to substitute healthy fresh produce in your meal instead of a heavy, rich sauce. The squash in this dish adds a glorious sunny color to the sauce, almost as bright as processed versions, and a great deal of vitamins A and C and fiber. The trick to a velvety sauce is making sure the squash is cooked long enough to purée silky smooth.

MAKE AHEAD

PREP TIME
10 MINUTES

COOK TIME
55 MINUTES

⅓ cup skim milk

½ cup (3 ounces) diced butternut squash

½ cup shredded low-fat Cheddar cheese

Pinch dry mustard

8 ounces (4 cups) cooked whole-wheat penne

1 tablespoon freshly grated Parmesan

PER SERVING
Calories: 446
Fat: 14.4g
Saturated fat: 8.2g
Protein: 22.4g
Carbohydrates: 53.7g
Sodium: 429mg
Fiber: 6.1g
Sugar: 4.5g

1. Preheat the oven to 350°F.

2. Combine the milk and squash in a large saucepan, and place it over medium-high heat. Bring the milk to a boil and then reduce the heat to low. Simmer until the squash is very tender, about 25 minutes. Remove the saucepan from the heat.

3. Pour the squash mixture into a blender. Purée and then pour it back into the saucepan. Add the Cheddar and mustard, stirring to melt. Stir in the penne, mixing thoroughly.

4. Transfer the pasta mixture to a 6-by-6-inch baking dish and sprinkle the top with the Parmesan. Bake until bubbly and lightly browned, about 20 minutes.

TIP: *You can put this casserole together in the morning, or even the night before, and simply pop it in the oven when you get home from work. If you are baking it directly from the refrigerator, add about 15 minutes to the cooking time.*

PAIR WITH . . . Broccoli with Lemon Butter (page 188)

Baked Ziti and Summer Squash

Casseroles are homey and feel like they should be put on the table in winter weather. This pretty, herb-flecked dish seems more like summer, with its creamy sauce, summer squash, and chunks of ripe tomato. This dish is a great make-ahead option because it can be thrown together and then baked right from the refrigerator. Do not freeze this casserole, though, because the cottage cheese will become grainy when it is thawed.

1. Preheat the oven to 400°F. Spray a 6-by-6-inch baking dish with the cooking spray.

2. Heat the olive oil in a large skillet over medium-high heat. Sauté the zucchini, scallion, and garlic until softened, about 2 minutes. Add the tomato and sauté for another 3 minutes. Remove the skillet from the heat and stir in the remaining ingredients until well mixed.

3. Spoon the pasta mixture into the baking dish. Bake until bubbly and lightly browned, about 15 minutes.

TIP: *If you have a gluten sensitivity, replace the ziti with your favorite gluten-free product. The cooking time for the whole-wheat casserole should be exactly the same because you are using cooked pasta.*

PAIR WITH . . . Wilted Greens (page 189)

Nonstick cooking spray
1 teaspoon olive oil
2 cups chopped zucchini (about 1 large)
1 scallion, white and green parts, sliced
1 teaspoon minced garlic
1 tomato, chopped
½ cup fat-free shredded Cheddar
2 tablespoons fat-free cottage cheese
1 egg, beaten
1 tablespoon chopped fresh basil or 1½ teaspoons dried basil
1 tablespoon chopped fresh oregano or 1 teaspoon dried oregano
Pinch sea salt
Pinch red pepper flakes
4 cups cooked whole-wheat ziti

PER SERVING
Calories: 313
Fat: 6.0g
Saturated fat: 1.2g
Protein: 16.1g
Carbohydrates: 52.1g
Sodium: 288mg
Fiber: 4.9g
Sugar: 6.7g

Spiced Eggplant Tagine

PREP TIME
15 MINUTES

COOK TIME
2 HOURS

It is unusual for a recipe to be named after the dish you traditionally cook it in, but that is exactly what you see here. A tagine is a North African conical ceramic cooking vessel designed to produce mouthwateringly tender meats and vegetables in a moist environment that keeps all the flavors in the pot. The conelike lid allows the released steam to rise up to the peak, condense, and trickle down the slanting sides back into the stew. Imagine the richness of flavor when not even a drop of taste is lost. Although this recipe is made in the oven, the cooking process is like what happens in a tagine, and so it still packs a tasty punch. Harissa is a spicy North African condiment made from peppers and other spices, and is available in the international aisle of many supermarkets.

1 eggplant, cut into ½-inch cubes
1 tomato, chopped
1 red bell pepper, seeded, deribbed, and julienned
½ onion, chopped
1 teaspoon minced garlic
1 tablespoon olive oil
½ teaspoon ground cumin
½ teaspoon ground coriander
¼ teaspoon ground turmeric
Pinch allspice
Pinch cayenne
½ cup low-sodium vegetable stock
1 teaspoon harissa
¼ cup coarsely chopped fresh parsley
2 lemon wedges

1. Preheat the oven to 300°F.

2. Combine the eggplant, tomato, bell pepper, onion, and garlic in a large lidded casserole dish. Drizzle the vegetables with the olive oil and toss them with the cumin, coriander, turmeric, allspice, and cayenne. Add the stock.

3. Cover and bake for 2 hours, until the vegetables are very tender. Remove from the oven and stir in the harissa. Serve topped with the parsley and lemon wedges.

TIP: *If you have leftover tagine, spoon it into a blender and pulse until it is a chunky purée. Use this savory, rich mixture as a dip for baked pita chips.*

PAIR WITH . . . Bulgur Herb Pilaf (page 194)

PER SERVING
Calories: 184
Fat: 8.5g
Saturated fat: 1.1g
Protein: 4.5g
Carbohydrates: 26.6g
Sodium: 114mg
Fiber: 11.2g
Sugar: 12.3g

Sweet Potato Cakes

This golden dish is like a vegetarian "meat loaf" using chickpeas and starchy vegetables instead of beef or chicken as a base. The patties are filling and have a pleasing, earthy sweetness from the sweet potatoes. You could combine them with almost any sauce or topping because the desired taste is not intense. This recipe can also be used if you want a nice "meatball" for a tomato-based pasta dish; simply punch up the seasoning with fresh oregano or basil, and roll the sweet potato mixture instead of creating burgerlike patties.

1. Preheat the oven to 400°F.

2. Heat 1 teaspoon of olive oil in a large skillet over medium-high heat. Sauté the onion and garlic until softened, about 2 minutes. Stir in the sweet potato and sauté for an additional 2 minutes. Remove from the heat.

3. Transfer to a food processor. Add the chickpeas, bread crumbs, lime juice, and egg white to the processor. Pulse until the chickpeas are ground and the mixture holds together. Divide the sweet potato mixture into two equal 4-inch patties, flattening them to about ¾ inch.

4. Heat the remaining 2 teaspoons of olive oil in a skillet. Cook the patties until browned, about 3 minutes on each side. Place the skillet in the oven and bake for an additional 5 minutes.

TIP: *Try doubling this easy recipe and having sweet potato cakes on ciabatta buns with Creamy Cucumber Salad (page 29) and shredded lettuce for lunch the next day. These cakes also freeze well wrapped tightly in plastic wrap; thaw them for a quick meal or snack.*

PAIR WITH . . . Creamy Mashed Cauliflower (page 189)

1 tablespoon olive oil, divided

¼ sweet onion, finely chopped

2 teaspoons minced garlic

1 peeled, grated sweet potato (about 1 cup)

1 cup sodium-free chickpeas, rinsed and drained

¼ cup whole-wheat bread crumbs

1 teaspoon freshly squeezed lime juice

1 egg white

Pinch sea salt

Pinch freshly ground black pepper

PER SERVING
Calories: 238
Fat: 8.3g
Saturated fat: 1.2g
Protein: 7.9g
Carbohydrates: 34.7g
Sodium: 270mg
Fiber: 5.3g
Sugar: 5.1g

Root Vegetable Curry

GLUTEN-FREE
DAIRY-FREE
MAKE AHEAD
30 MINUTES
ONE-POT

PREP TIME
10 MINUTES

COOK TIME
20 MINUTES

Starchy root vegetables come in an assortment of textures and tastes, so mix and match to find appealing combinations. Root vegetables are budget-friendly ingredients; an entire pot of this curry might set you back only a few dollars. This recipe is a tomato-based curry, but you could replace the vegetable stock with coconut milk for a creamier version of this dish. In that case, try to get a light coconut milk rather than full fat one.

1 teaspoon olive oil

2 shallots, peeled and diced

½ teaspoon minced garlic

1 tablespoon curry powder or paste

1 parsnip, peeled and cut into 1-inch chunks

1 sweet potato, peeled and diced

1 carrot, peeled and cut into 1-inch chunks

1 cup canned lentils, rinsed and drained

1 tomato, chopped

½ cup low-sodium vegetable stock

PER SERVING
Calories: 321
Fat: 4.3g
Saturated fat: 0.0g
Protein: 16.5g
Carbohydrates: 57.9g
Sodium: 88mg
Fiber: 14.7g
Sugar: 11.0g

1. Heat the olive oil in a large saucepan over medium-high heat. Sauté the shallots and garlic until softened, about 2 minutes. Add the curry powder and sauté for an additional minute.

2. Add the remaining ingredients and bring the stew to a boil. Reduce the heat to low and simmer until the vegetables are tender, about 15 minutes.

TIP: *Sweet potatoes add rich color to any dish, along with more than 200 percent of the daily recommended amount (RDA) of vitamin A and 50 percent of the RDA of vitamin C. Sweet potatoes are also a fabulous source of beta-carotene, which is a powerful disease fighter, so make this root vegetable a regular ingredient in your healthy diet.*

PAIR WITH . . . Quinoa Primavera (page 193)

PREP TIME
10 MINUTES

COOK TIME
15 MINUTES

Tomato Indian Stew

Fresh ginger provides the majority of the flavor in this easy dish, along with powerful health benefits. Ginger is a centuries-old remedy for digestive ailments, which explains the practice of drinking ginger ale when your tummy is upset. Ginger looks like a bulbous root, but it is actually a rhizome, which is a type of underground stem. Ginger can also help treat arthritis pain and protect against some cancers, such as ovarian cancer. Ginger should be a staple ingredient in your healthy-eating pantry, so you always have it on hand for sauces, dressings, soups, juices, and desserts.

1. Heat the olive oil in a large skillet over medium-high heat. Add the onion and garlic, and sauté until the vegetables are softened, about 4 minutes. Stir in the ginger, cumin, and coriander and cook, stirring, until the spices are very fragrant, about 1 minute.

2. Add the crushed tomatoes, chickpeas, tomato, and stock. Bring to a boil; then reduce the heat to low and simmer until the sauce thickens, about 10 minutes. Serve topped with the yogurt and cilantro.

TIP: *Fresh ginger has a milder taste than its powdered counterpart, so don't panic at the amount used in this recipe. You can store unused fresh ginger in the refrigerator for up to three weeks if it is unpeeled.*

PAIR WITH . . . Banana Basmati Rice (page 194)

1 teaspoon olive oil

1 sweet onion, finely chopped

1 teaspoon minced garlic

1 teaspoon peeled, grated fresh ginger

1 teaspoon ground cumin

½ teaspoon ground coriander

1 (15-ounce) can low-sodium crushed tomatoes

1 (15-ounce) can sodium-free canned chickpeas, rinsed and drained

1 tomato, diced

½ cup low-sodium vegetable stock

2 tablespoons low-fat plain Greek yogurt

2 tablespoons chopped fresh cilantro

PER SERVING
Calories: 266
Fat: 4.4g
Saturated fat: 0.6g
Protein: 14.8g
Carbohydrates: 42.0g
Sodium: 517mg
Fiber: 14.1g
Sugar: 14.3g

Curried Chickpea Stew

GLUTEN-FREE
MAKE AHEAD
30 MINUTES
ONE-POT

PREP TIME
15 MINUTES

COOK TIME
10 MINUTES

Curry is a staple vegetarian dish in many cultures. Most vegetarian ingredients, such as tofu, vegetables, grains, beans, fruit, and eggs, pair superbly with curry spices. Curry powder is a combination of many different spices in varying quantities; in some countries, each household has their own special blend. Experiment with bottled curry powders and recipes; once you learn the basics, you can easily create a blend that suits your heat tolerance and palate. Since there are so many herbs and spices in curry, it should come as no surprise that curry dishes have many health benefits. Curry can help boost your immune system, reduce the risk of cancer and cardiovascular disease, and elevate your mood. It can also increase your energy levels.

1 teaspoon olive oil

1 onion, chopped

½ teaspoon minced garlic

1 teaspoon curry powder

½ teaspoon ground cumin

½ teaspoon ground coriander

1 (15-ounce) can chickpeas, rinsed and drained

2 tomatoes, chopped

½ cup spinach, shredded

2 tablespoons fat-free plain Greek yogurt

PER SERVING
Calories: 313
Fat: 6.0g
Saturated fat: 1.2g
Protein: 16.1g
Carbohydrates: 52.1g
Sodium: 288mg
Fiber: 4.9g
Sugar: 6.7g

1. Heat the olive oil in a medium saucepan over medium-high heat. Sauté the onion and garlic until softened, about 2 minutes. Add the curry powder, cumin, and coriander, and sauté for an additional 2 minutes.

2. Add the chickpeas and tomatoes and cook, stirring, until the chickpeas are heated through and the sauce thickens, about 5 minutes. Add the spinach and sauté until it wilts, about 1 minute. Remove from the heat and stir in the yogurt.

TIP: *You can use curry paste instead of the dried spices and adjust the heat according to your palate. Remember that curry often mellows as it sits.*

PAIR WITH . . . Pistachio Rice Pilaf (page 194)

GLUTEN-FREE
DAIRY-FREE
MAKE AHEAD
30 MINUTES
ONE-POT

PREP TIME
5 MINUTES

COOK TIME
25 MINUTES

Red Lentil Quinoa Stew

Quinoa is a very popular side dish and salad ingredient, but it is not usually seen in soups and stews, because it is a very small grain. In this dish, the quinoa and lentils create a thick, slightly spicy sauce for the vegetables. Red lentils are a better aesthetic choice here than green ones, and the taste is the same regardless of color.

1. Heat the olive oil in a large saucepan over medium-high heat. Sauté the onion, celery, and garlic until softened, about 3 minutes. Add the vegetable stock, carrot, tomato, lentils, and quinoa. Bring to a boil; then reduce the heat to low. Simmer the stew until the vegetables and lentils are tender and the quinoa is cooked, 15 to 20 minutes.

2. Remove from the heat and stir in the thyme and chili flakes. Season with salt and pepper. Serve topped with the parsley.

TIP: *Always rinse quinoa well. The natural saponins that coat this grain can taste bitter or cause stomach upset. Rinse twice, or until the water shows no white, soapy foam, to ensure the saponins are dissolved. Some packaged quinoa has already been rinsed, though, so follow the directions on the package.*

PAIR WITH . . . Fresh Gingered Melon (page 198)

1 teaspoon olive oil
½ onion, chopped
1 celery stalk, diced
1 teaspoon minced garlic
2 cups low-sodium vegetable stock
1 carrot, peeled and diced
1 tomato, diced
½ cup red lentils, rinsed
¼ cup quinoa, rinsed
1 tablespoon chopped fresh thyme or 1 teaspoon dried thyme
Pinch hot pepper flakes
Sea salt
Freshly ground black pepper
1 tablespoon chopped fresh parsley

PER SERVING
Calories: 315
Fat: 4.4g
Saturated fat: 0.6g
Protein: 17.7g
Carbohydrates: 53.0g
Sodium: 637mg
Fiber: 18.8g
Sugar: 7.7g

CHAPTER 6

Fish and Seafood

Halibut with Wilted Greens

PREP TIME
5 MINUTES

COOK TIME
15 MINUTES

Even if you are not an accomplished cook, you'll surprise yourself with this incredibly simple preparation. What could be easier than layering fresh greens with halibut and letting the oven's heat and the fish's natural juices do all the work? This recipe is so foolproof you can do all the prep in about five minutes in the morning between packing a lunch and brushing your teeth. When you get home from work, simply preheat your oven while you get into your comfy clothes and bake the halibut straight from the refrigerator. Add five extra minutes if you follow this make-ahead method.

1. Preheat the oven to 375°F. Lightly coat an 8-by-8-inch baking dish with cooking spray.

2. Layer the spinach and Swiss chard in the bottom of the baking dish. Top the greens with the cherry tomatoes, and place the fish in the baking dish skin-side up. Drizzle the fish with the olive oil and lemon juice. Sprinkle the lemon zest and thyme over the fish.

3. Bake until the fish flakes easily, about 15 minutes. Season with salt and pepper.

TIP: *Leave the fish skin on during baking. The skin helps the flesh stay moist because it acts as an insulating layer between the heat of the oven and the meat of the fish. The skin often imparts flavor as well, even if you peel it off before your meal.*

PAIR WITH . . . Herbed Egg Noodles (page 192)

Nonstick cooking spray

1 cup spinach leaves

1 cup Swiss chard

10 cherry tomatoes, halved

2 (5-ounce) boneless, skin-on halibut fillets

1 teaspoon olive oil

Juice and zest of ½ lemon

1 tablespoon chopped fresh thyme or 1 teaspoon dried thyme

Sea salt

Freshly ground black pepper

PER SERVING

Calories: 195
Fat: 5.7g
Saturated fat: 0.9g
Protein: 31.1g
Carbohydrates: 5.6g
Sodium: 255mg
Fiber: 1.8g
Sugar: 2.3g

Tomato-Baked Halibut

Much of the guesswork involved in preparing fish is eliminated when you simply bake it in a thick tomato sauce. There is no direct heat to dry out the flesh, and the fish remains intact because you don't have to move it with tongs or a spatula. You can prepare this dish for baking the day before. Just make sure to allow the tomato sauce to cool completely before spooning it onto the raw fish.

PREP TIME
5 MINUTES

COOK TIME
20 MINUTES

Nonstick cooking spray

2 (5-ounce) boneless, skinless halibut fillets

1 teaspoon olive oil

½ sweet onion, cut into ⅛-inch-thick slices

½ teaspoon minced garlic

2 tomatoes, chopped

6 sun-dried tomatoes, chopped

Pinch freshly ground black pepper

1 tablespoon chopped fresh thyme, or 1 teaspoon dried thyme

PER SERVING
Calories: 279
Fat: 7.1g
Saturated fat: 1.0g
Protein: 40.6g
Carbohydrates: 13.2g
Sodium: 233mg
Fiber: 3.9g
Sugar: 7.8g

1. Preheat the oven to 400°F. Lightly coat an 8-by-8-inch baking dish with cooking spray.

2. Place the fish fillets in the dish. Set aside.

3. Heat the olive oil in a skillet over medium heat. Sauté the onion and garlic until softened, about 3 minutes. Stir in the tomatoes and sun-dried tomatoes, and cook for 5 minutes. Remove from the heat and season with pepper.

4. Spoon the tomato mixture over the fish in the baking dish. Bake until the fish flakes easily, about 8 minutes. Remove from the oven and serve topped with the thyme.

TIP: *If you are using sun-dried tomatoes that are not packed in oil, it can be difficult to chop them. Try using a pair of kitchen shears instead to snip the tomatoes into small pieces.*

PAIR WITH . . . Parmesan-Sautéed Zucchini (page 192)

Teriyaki Salmon with Ginger

PREP TIME
5 MINUTES
(+ marinating time)

COOK TIME
6 MINUTES

Teriyaki sauce does not have to be complicated or unhealthy. Teriyaki refers to the cooking technique involving in grilling or broiling foods in a soy-mirin glaze. Mirin is a rice wine with a high sugar content and low alcohol level, which makes it perfect for creating a caramel-like sheen on fish and meats. This recipe uses honey instead of mirin because it is more commonly available. If you want to try a more traditional preparation, you can find mirin in most grocery stores or Asian markets.

1. In a small bowl, stir together the honey, tamari, and ginger until well blended.

2. Place the salmon in a baking dish and spoon the sauce over it, spreading it out. Cover the dish and let the salmon marinate for at least 30 minutes in the refrigerator.

3. Preheat the oven to 350°F. Line a baking pan with aluminum foil.

4. Place the salmon in the baking pan and spoon any leftover marinade over the fish. Bake until the salmon is opaque, about 12 minutes.

TIP: *If you tend to use a lot of fresh ginger in your meals, it is a good idea to get a Microplane grater. This handy mini kitchen tool can reduce the most fibrous ginger to a smooth, uniform paste.*

PAIR WITH . . . Sautéed Mixed Vegetables (page 190)

2 tablespoons honey
2 tablespoons low-sodium tamari sauce
1 teaspoon peeled, grated fresh ginger
2 (6-ounce) skinless salmon fillets

PER SERVING
Calories: 388
Fat: 18.1g
Saturated fat: 3.8g
Protein: 35.3g
Carbohydrates: 18.9g
Sodium: 799mg
Fiber: 0.0g
Sugar: 18.3g

Honeyed Sesame Salmon

GLUTEN-FREE
DAIRY-FREE
MAKE AHEAD
30 MINUTES

Salmon lends itself well to sweet flavorings, and the honey in the marinade can create a gorgeous golden crust on the fish. Honey is also naturally acidic, which can help break down the surface proteins in the salmon to create a tender finished product. Try different types of honey, such as malty buckwheat, delicately floral clover, or smoky mesquite, to enjoy interesting variations on this simple recipe.

PREP TIME
5 MINUTES

COOK TIME
15 MINUTES
(not counting marinating time)

2 (6-ounce) skinless
    salmon fillets
2 tablespoons honey
Sea salt
Freshly ground black pepper
2 tablespoons sesame seeds

PER SERVING
Calories: 361
Fat: 17.3g
Saturated fat: 2.5g
Protein: 34.7g
Carbohydrates: 19.4g
Sodium: 194mg
Fiber: 1.1g
Sugar: 17.3g

1. Place the salmon and honey in a resealable plastic bag and marinate in the refrigerator for at least 1 hour.

2. Preheat the oven to 350°F.

3. Place the salmon and any juices from the bag in a small 8-by-8-inch baking dish and season with salt and pepper. Bake until the salmon is opaque and flakes with a fork, about 12 minutes. Serve topped with the sesame seeds.

TIP: *To enhance the nutty flavor of the sesame seeds, try toasting them in a small skillet on the stove. Place them in a skillet over medium heat and swirl them in the pan until they brown and become very fragrant.*

PAIR WITH . . . Mashed Roasted Butternut Squash (page 192)

GLUTEN-FREE
DAIRY-FREE
MAKE AHEAD
30 MINUTES
ONE-POT

PREP TIME
5 MINUTES

COOK TIME
12 MINUTES

Salmon with Sun-Dried Tomato Pesto

You will not believe how flavorful salmon becomes when roasted under a cap of rich sun-dried tomato pesto. Drying tomatoes concentrates all the sweet, fragrant goodness of this fruit by removing the water content, while preserving the nutrients. Sun-dried tomatoes are a good source of protein, iron, and vitamin K. When not packed in oil, they are low in calories, as well.

1. Preheat the oven to 350°F. Line a small baking pan with aluminum foil.

2. Place the salmon fillets on the baking sheet and spread 1 tablespoon of pesto on each piece of fish. Bake until the fish is opaque, about 12 minutes.

3. Serve with lemon wedges.

TIP: *If you want to make your own pesto with sun-dried tomatoes that have not been preserved in olive oil, reconstitute the sun-dried tomatoes by soaking them in hot water for a few minutes; this will plump them up enough to purée in a blender or food processor.*

PAIR WITH . . . Roasted Cauliflower (page 189)

2 (6-ounce) skinless salmon fillets

2 tablespoons store-bought sun-dried tomato pesto

½ lemon, cut into 4 wedges

PER SERVING
Calories: 250
Fat: 12.0g
Saturated fat: 1.9g
Protein: 33.5g
Carbohydrates: 2.3g
Sodium: 218mg
Fiber: 0.5g
Sugar: 1.2g

Herbed Salmon Burgers

GLUTEN-FREE
DAIRY-FREE
MAKE AHEAD
30 MINUTES

PREP TIME
10 MINUTES
COOK TIME
10 MINUTES

These juicy burgers have a distinct Asian flair with the addition of tamari sauce, ginger, and smoky sesame oil. Even when chopped, salmon has such a firm texture that creates a meaty feel in these burgers. It is packed full of healthy nutrients, including vitamin D, which is not usually found in foods. Try to source wild salmon whenever possible because it is a glorious natural rosy color and high in disease-busting antioxidants and anti-inflammatory components.

1 tablespoon low-sodium tamari sauce

½ teaspoon honey

1 (½-pound) skinless salmon fillet, chopped into ¼-inch pieces

1 scallion, white and green parts, finely chopped

1 egg white, lightly beaten

1 tablespoon peeled, grated fresh ginger

½ teaspoon toasted sesame oil

Nonstick cooking spray

PER SERVING
Calories: 193
Fat: 8.3g
Saturated fat: 1.2g
Protein: 25.2g
Carbohydrates: 4.5g
Sodium: 435mg
Fiber: 0.5g
Sugar: 1.8g

1. In a small bowl, stir together the tamari and honey until well blended. Set aside.

2. In a medium bowl, thoroughly mix the salmon, scallion, egg white, ginger, and sesame oil. Form the salmon mixture into two patties about 1 inch thick.

3. Place a medium skillet over medium-high heat and coat it lightly with the cooking spray. Cook the patties for 4 minutes per side, or until they are cooked through. Brush the glaze over the burgers and cook for 1 additional minute per side.

TIP: *If you are sensitive to gluten, use tamari sauce instead of soy sauce, which usually contains gluten. As with any ingredient, make sure you check the label for potential allergens. While most tamari is gluten-free, always be sure. Tamari sauce works well in most recipes that call for soy sauce. Even though it is less salty, it has a richer taste.*

PAIR WITH . . . Green Beans with Pecans (page 190)

Grouper with Black Olive Tomato Sauce

This sauce is reminiscent of puttanesca pasta sauce, though without the anchovies found in many traditional recipes. The salty taste from the olives is a perfect accompaniment for the mild grouper. Grouper's pleasingly firm texture is similar to halibut. If you can't find fresh grouper, then halibut is an acceptable substitute.

1. Season the grouper with salt and pepper.

2. Put a large skillet over medium-high heat and coat it lightly with the cooking spray. Cook the fish for 5 minutes per side, or until the fish flakes easily. Set aside.

3. Put a small skillet over medium-high heat and coat it with cooking spray. Sauté the scallion and garlic until softened, about 3 minutes. Add the oregano, tomato, and olives to the skillet and cook, stirring, about 6 minutes.

4. Serve the grouper topped with the tomato mixture and chopped parsley.

TIP: *Real Kalamata olives come from a region in Greece by the same name. Look for olives that are dark brown in color rather than true black. Before this beautiful fruit is brined, it is an unmistakable dark purple hue. You can use other olives in this dish, but your sauce won't be quite as rich.*

PAIR WITH . . . Simple Roasted Baby Potatoes (page 191)

2 (6-ounce) grouper fillets
Pinch sea salt
Pinch freshly ground
  black pepper
Nonstick cooking spray
1 scallion, white and green
  parts, thinly sliced
1 teaspoon minced garlic
1 tablespoon chopped fresh
  oregano or 1 teaspoon
  dried oregano
2 tomatoes, chopped
2 tablespoons chopped, pitted
  Kalamata olives
2 tablespoons chopped fresh
  parsley

PER SERVING
Calories: 266
Fat: 5.4g
Saturated fat: 0.9g
1.0g Protein: 44.4g
Carbohydrates: 9.4g
Sodium: 293mg
Fiber: 3.2g
Sugar: 5.0g

Cod with Pesto Vegetables in Parchment

GLUTEN-FREE
DAIRY-FREE
MAKE AHEAD
30 MINUTES

This cooking method is a classic French technique called *en papillote*, and it is one of the healthiest ways to make your meals when you get the hang of all the paper folding. Once you cook in parchment, you will want to think up a slew of dishes that you can fold in paper. There is something festive about opening your own individual parchment packet, almost like getting a delicious present. This method is also perfect for cooking for couples or single portions, because there is little waste and each meal is completely self-contained.

PREP TIME
15 MINUTES

COOK TIME
15 MINUTES

Nonstick cooking spray

1 carrot, peeled and shredded

1 zucchini, shredded

1 red bell pepper, seeded, deribbed, and julienned

1 tablespoon prepared or homemade pesto

2 (6-ounce) cod fillets

¼ teaspoon freshly ground black pepper

2 teaspoons chicken stock or dry white wine

PER SERVING

Calories: 309
Fat: 7.7g
Saturated fat: 1.1g
Protein: 48.0g
Carbohydrates: 10.2g
Sodium: 212mg
Fiber: 3.3g
Sugar: 5.7g

1. Preheat the oven to 450°F.

2. Cut two 12-by-18-inch sheets of parchment paper. Spread the parchment on the work surface and spray lightly with the cooking spray.

3. In a small bowl, toss the vegetables with the pesto until evenly coated. Evenly divide the vegetables between the two pieces of parchment, placing them in a mound in the middle of the paper. Place a fish fillet on top of each mound. Season each fillet with half the pepper and drizzle with the stock.

4. Fold the edges of the parchment together to create a package and fold the ends under so the package is sealed. Place the parchment packets on a baking sheet.

5. Bake for 15 minutes. Open the packets and transfer the fish fillets and vegetables to plates.

6. Pour the juices over the top and serve.

TIP: *The trick to creating successful perfectly cooked meals* en papillote *is to cut up the vegetables evenly and thinly. It is also important to completely seal the packets and not peek during the cooking time, so the steam stays trapped.*

PAIR WITH . . . Garlic Quinoa (page 193)

Simple Spinach-Baked Sole

If you love traditional sole Florentine, this healthier, quicker recipe might be your new special-occasion dish. Instead of being drenched in a creamy cheese sauce, this fish has a light layer of Parmesan cheese, which cuts down the calories and fat. This less-rich version allows the delicate, mild fish to shine through. Sole has very little oil in it naturally, so the quick-cooking method in this recipe ensures that your fish will not dry out.

1. Preheat the oven to 400°F.

2. Place a large skillet over medium-high heat and lightly coat it with the cooking spray. Add the spinach and sauté until wilted, about 3 minutes. Transfer the spinach to a sieve and press out any excess water. Spread in an 8-by-8-inch baking dish.

3. Arrange the sole fillets over the spinach. Top with the scallion and carrot. Season with salt and pepper. Sprinkle with the Parmesan.

4. Bake until the fish is cooked through and the cheese is lightly browned, about 15 minutes.

TIP: *You should always make sure you buy sustainably produced fish whenever possible: Look for the Marine Stewardship Council label on the packaging. This ensures you are supporting the health of the world's oceans for a better future.*

PAIR WITH . . . Simple Roasted Baby Potatoes (page 191)

Nonstick cooking spray
5 cups packed spinach
2 sole fillets
1 scallion, white and green parts, chopped
1 cup shredded carrot
Sea salt
Freshly ground black pepper
¼ cup grated Parmesan cheese

PER SERVING
Calories 281
Fat: 8.4g
Saturated fat: 4.5g
Protein: 42.5g
Carbohydrates: 9.6g
Sodium: 609mg
Fiber: 3.4g
Sugar: 3.1g

Sole with Cucumber Salsa

DAIRY-FREE
30 MINUTES

PREP TIME
15 MINUTES

COOK TIME
6 MINUTES

If you have an eye on living a longer, healthier life, fish should be part of your meals at least two or three times a week. Fish is a low-fat, high-protein ingredient that seems to cry out for fresh, simple preparations. What is more fresh and cool than a salsa created from cucumber and flavored with herbs and tart lemon juice? The fish in this recipe is lightly dredged in flour and panfried to create a golden crispy crust, sealing in the juicy, tender flesh. If you want a gluten-free meal, skip the dredging and just season the sole with a little freshly ground black pepper before placing it in the skillet.

2 cups diced English cucumber

8 cherry tomatoes, quartered

½ scallion, white and green parts, finely chopped

1 tablespoon chopped fresh coriander

1 teaspoon freshly squeezed lemon juice

Sea salt

Freshly ground black pepper

¼ cup all-purpose flour

2 (7-ounce) sole fillets

1 teaspoon olive oil

1. In a small bowl, combine the cucumber, tomato, scallion, coriander, and lemon juice. Season with salt and pepper.

2. Place the flour on a plate and dredge the fish in it, coating both sides.

3. Heat the olive oil in a large skillet over medium-high heat. Cook the sole until it is golden brown, about 2 minutes per side. Serve immediately with the cucumber salsa.

TIP: *If you use field cucumbers instead of English cucumbers, peel off the skin and scoop out the seeds with a spoon.*

PAIR WITH . . . Sautéed Mixed Vegetables (page 190)

PER SERVING
Calories: 346
Fat: 5.5g
Saturated fat: 1.3g
Protein: 43.6g
Carbohydrates: 35.2g
Sodium: 214mg
Fiber: 7.1g
Sugar: 12.9g

Oven-Baked Fish and Chips

PREP TIME
20 MINUTES

COOK TIME
30 MINUTES

Traditional English-style fish and chips are a culinary masterpiece that can take years to perfect. Imagine buttery-smooth cod or haddock encased in a crispy, golden batter sitting proudly on heaps of thick, seasoned potato wedges. Heavenly, but also artery clogging. In this version, the fish is golden-crisp. Baking the breaded fish and potatoes in the oven eliminates the calories and fat added from deep-frying , while preserving the satisfying richness of this pub favorite.

1. Preheat the oven to 425°F. Lightly coat a baking sheet with the cooking spray. Place a wire cooling rack on another small baking sheet and spray the rack with cooking spray.

2. Pat the potato wedges completely dry with paper towels and transfer them to a medium bowl. Toss the potatoes with the olive oil and paprika. Spread the wedges on the prepared baking sheet. Bake the potatoes for about 30 minutes, until golden and crispy, turning several times.

3. While the potatoes are baking, put the cornflakes on a plate, combine the flour and salt on another plate, and put the egg in a bowl between the plates to form a battering station. Batter the fish by dredging it in the flour mixture, dipping it in the egg, and then dredging it in the cornflakes. Place the battered fish on the prepared wire rack. Spray both sides of the fish with cooking spray.

4. Bake the fish with the potatoes until it is cooked through and the batter is golden and crisp, about 15 to 20 minutes. Serve hot with the lemon wedges.

TIP: *Breading food is a messy process that can create thickly breaded fingers. Try using the two-hand method employed by chefs. Designate one hand your "wet" hand and the other one the "dry" hand. Use the dry hand to flour and pack on the bread crumbs, and the wet hand to dip the fish in the egg.*

PAIR WITH . . . Tropical Fruit Salad with Creamy Lime Sauce (page 198)

Nonstick cooking spray

2 potatoes, skin on and cut into ¼-inch-thick wedges

2 teaspoons olive oil

½ teaspoon hot or smoked paprika

1 cup finely crushed cornflakes

2 tablespoons all-purpose flour

Pinch sea salt

1 egg, beaten

2 (5-ounce) cod fillets

½ lemon, cut into wedges

PER SERVING
Calories: 447
Fat: 8.4g
Saturated fat: 1.7g
Protein: 40.6g
Carbohydrates: 51.9g
Sodium: 371mg
Fiber: 6.0g
Sugar: 4.2g

Shrimp and Fresh Pea Fettuccine

DAIRY-FREE
30 MINUTES
ONE-POT

PREP TIME
10 MINUTES

COOK TIME
10 MINUTES

Figuring out which shrimp at the grocery store are small, medium, or large can be tricky, especially if you don't know what "count" means with respect to shrimp. The count refers to the number of shrimp found in a pound; the smaller the number, such as 16/18, the larger the shrimp. The shrimp in this dish are small enough to be a succulent mouthful but big enough to have a visual impact. It can be pretty to leave the tails on your shrimp, but it can make eating the pasta a bit more difficult.

1 teaspoon olive oil

1½ teaspoons minced garlic

16 medium (31/35 count) shrimp, peeled and deveined

½ cup low-sodium chicken stock

4 sweet peppers, sliced

¾ cup fresh or frozen peas

½ teaspoon lemon zest

½ teaspoon chopped fresh thyme or ¼ teaspoon dried thyme

Pinch freshly ground black pepper

1 tablespoon chopped fresh parsley or 1 teaspoon dried parsley

3 cups cooked spinach fettuccine

1. Heat the olive oil in a large skillet over medium-high heat. Sauté the garlic until fragrant, about 1 minute. Add the shrimp and the chicken stock. Sauté until the shrimp turn opaque, about 4 minutes.

2. Stir in the peas, sweet peppers, lemon zest, thyme, and pepper, and sauté for 1 minute. Add the parsley and fettuccine and toss until the pasta is heated through, about 2 minutes.

TIP: *Flavored pastas used to be a special order and only available fresh, but now you can find dried spinach, tomato, and lemon pepper pastas in the Italian food section of most supermarkets. Any flavor works well with the combination of ingredients in this dish.*

PAIR WITH . . . Citrus Curd with Berries (page 199)

PER SERVING
Calories: 419
Fat: 4.0g
Saturated fat: 0.6g
Protein: 47.0g
Carbohydrates: 44.8g
Sodium: 1,178mg
Fiber: 5.4g
Sugar: 2.8g

Ginger Shrimp with Soba Noodles

This simple dish pairs fresh asparagus and tender pink shrimp on a bed of tasty, spicy noodles. You might want to eat with chopsticks to get the full impact of this Asian-influenced recipe. Soba noodles are made with a buckwheat base and are often gluten-free; look for a product made with 100% buckwheat or with additional rice flour. However, many soba products contain wheat to stop the noodles from falling apart during the cooking process, so read the package ingredients carefully.

1. Cook the soba noodles according to the package directions. Add the asparagus in the last minute of cooking. Drain and run under cold water. Transfer the noodles and asparagus to a large bowl and set aside.

2. Whisk together the tamari sauce, vinegar, sesame oil, and honey in a medium bowl.

3. Add 1 tablespoon of the sauce to the noodles and toss to combine. Add the shrimp, ginger, and garlic to the remaining tamari mixture, and mix well.

4. Heat the olive oil in a medium skillet over medium-high heat. Sauté the shrimp mixture for about 4 minutes, until the shrimp are cooked through and lightly browned. Add the shrimp to the noodles and asparagus and serve topped with the scallion.

TIP: *Look for bright-green asparagus about as wide as a pencil or thinner with tightly closed tips for the finest taste and texture. If you find thin, tender stalks, cut off about 1 inch at the bottom and use the rest in your recipe.*

PAIR WITH . . . Sesame Green Beans (page 189)

3 ounces dried soba noodles

16 asparagus spears, trimmed of woody ends and cut into 2-inch pieces

1 teaspoon tamari sauce

1 teaspoon rice wine vinegar

½ teaspoon sesame oil

½ teaspoon honey

10 medium (31/35 count) shrimp, peeled and deveined

1 teaspoon peeled, grated fresh ginger

1 teaspoon minced garlic

1 teaspoon olive oil

1 scallion, white and green parts, thinly sliced

PER SERVING

Calories: 367
Fat: 5.9g
Saturated fat: 1.2g
Protein: 36.7g
Carbohydrates: 44.4g
Sodium: 961mg
Fiber: 4.4g
Sugar: 5.8g

Chili Shrimp

GLUTEN-FREE
DAIRY-FREE
MAKE AHEAD
30 MINUTES

PREP TIME
10 MINUTES
(+ marinating time)
COOK TIME
6 MINUTES

Sizzling, juicy, spice-flecked shrimp on skewers seem undeniably decadent, especially when savored on a sultry summer evening in the company of a special person in your life. These piquant beauties should be eaten with your hands, so leave the tails on to give you something to hold. Just make sure you have lots of napkins on the table to mop your hands after dinner.

Juice and zest of 1 lime
1 teaspoon olive oil
1 teaspoon honey
½ teaspoon smoked paprika
¼ teaspoon chili powder
12 large (21/30 count) shrimp, peeled and deveined
Freshly ground black pepper
1 tablespoon chopped fresh cilantro

PER SERVING
Calories: 303
Fat: 2.5g
Saturated fat: 0.0g
Protein: 63.1g
Carbohydrates: 9.4g
Sodium: 424mg
Fiber: 0.0g
Sugar: 2.9g

1. Stir together the lime juice and zest, olive oil, honey, paprika, and chili powder in a medium bowl. Add the shrimp and toss to combine. Transfer the shrimp and marinade to a resealable freezer bag and refrigerate for at least 6 hours.

2. Preheat the grill to medium-high.

3. Thread 3 shrimp each on 4 wooden skewers that have been soaked for 30 minutes in water, and discard any remaining marinade. Grill the shrimp, turning once, until cooked through, about 6 minutes. Serve topped with the cilantro and freshly ground black pepper.

TIP: *Always soak wooden skewers for about 30 minutes so they don't burn during the grilling process. You can also use metal skewers if this dish is a regular addition to your meals. If you do not have a barbecue, preheat your oven to broil and place the shrimp on a small baking sheet. You don't have to put them on skewers. Broil the shrimp three minutes per side until sizzling and cooked through.*

PAIR WITH . . . Sweet Potato Parsnip Mash (page 191)

Spicy Seafood Ragù

PREP TIME
20 MINUTES

COOK TIME
20 MINUTES

Ragù usually means meat braised slowly in a sauce. This dish uses seafood instead of meat, and seafood does not need to be cooked slowly to be tender. Scallops, shrimp, and most fish need very little time in the sauce to pick up its spicy flavor and have the perfect texture. The heat in this recipe comes from the paprika, so it is important to make sure you do not buy the sweet variety. For an additional twist, however, you may substitute smoked paprika for a portion of the hot variety; however, this condiment is best used in small doses.

1. Heat 1 teaspoon of olive oil in a large skillet over medium heat. Sauté the halibut, scallops, and shrimp, stirring occasionally, until just opaque, about 3 minutes. Transfer the seafood to a plate and cover with aluminum foil to keep warm.

2. Add the remaining 2 teaspoons of olive oil and sauté the onion until lightly browned, 5 to 7 minutes. Increase the heat to medium-high. Add the oregano, basil, paprika, and pepper and sauté for 30 seconds.

3. Add the chicken stock, wine, and tomatoes and bring to a boil. Reduce the heat to low and simmer, stirring frequently, for 6 minutes. Add the seafood and potatoes to the skillet, and simmer until heated through, about 2 minutes. Serve garnished with the parsley.

TIP: *Scallops need to be cleaned before you use them, unless you buy them cleaned from your local fish counter. To clean them yourself, hold the scallop under cold running water and run your thumb across the entire surface to remove any grit. Detach any remaining side muscle pieces by feeling for tougher sections on the edges of the scallop. You will recognize the side muscle because the fiber in it runs in a different direction than the main body of the scallop.*

PAIR WITH . . . Broccoli with Lemon Butter (page 188)

1 tablespoon olive oil, divided
1 (5-ounce) halibut fillet, diced
8 bay scallops, patted dry
4 medium (31/35 count) shrimp, peeled, deveined, and chopped
½ sweet onion, diced
1 tablespoon chopped fresh oregano or 1 teaspoon dried oregano
1 tablespoon chopped fresh basil or 1 teaspoon dried basil
1 teaspoon hot paprika
¼ teaspoon freshly ground black pepper
1 cup low-sodium chicken stock
½ cup dry white wine
2 tomatoes, diced
6 new potatoes (2 inches in diameter), cooked and quartered
1 tablespoon chopped fresh parsley

PER SERVING
Calories: 388
Fat: 9.1g
Saturated fat: 1.5g
Protein: 37.8g
Carbohydrates: 29.1g
Sodium: 270mg
Fiber: 4.1g
Sugar: 5.5g

Chicken, Turkey, and Duck

Tangy Lemon Chicken

This tart-sweet chicken stir-fry would not be out of place in a neat cardboard box from a Chinese restaurant. It has an almost professional look and feel to it. Stir-frying is a speedy, efficient way to create a meal, and the prepared ingredients look lovely lined up and ready to go in the skillet or wok. Whenever you cook Asian-style meals, it is important to follow the order of ingredients because each different meat or vegetable takes varying times to cook. You wouldn't want to add an ingredient like snow peas first, because by the time everything else is done, your peas would be overcooked and grayish.

1. Place a large skillet or wok over medium-high heat and spray with the cooking spray. Add the chicken and sauté until it is just cooked through, about 4 minutes. Remove the chicken from the skillet with a slotted spoon and set it aside on a plate.

2. Reduce the heat to medium and add the onion, bell pepper, garlic, and ginger; sauté, stirring often, until the vegetables are softened, 5 to 6 minutes. Add the carrots and sauté for 2 minutes. Add the chicken stock and cook until liquid is simmering. Cover the skillet and simmer for 10 minutes, stirring occasionally.

3. In a small bowl, whisk together the flour and tamari sauce to make a smooth paste. Whisk in the lemon zest and juice.

4. Move the vegetables to the side of the skillet and whisk the flour mixture into the liquid in the skillet. Bring the liquid back to a boil, whisking constantly until thickened. Add the green beans and cook for 2 minutes. Stir the chicken back in and serve immediately.

TIP: *Be precise with the size of ingredients when stir-frying, because uniform cuts will help everything to cook evenly and quickly. A 2-inch broccoli floret will not become crisp-tender at the same time as a 1-inch floret. It also looks neater and more attractive to have uniform ingredients.*

PAIR WITH . . . Garlic Quinoa (page 193)

Nonstick cooking spray

1 (8-ounce) skinless, boneless chicken breast, cut into ¼-inch-thick slices

½ sweet onion, cut into ¼-inch-thick slices

1 red bell pepper, seeded, deribbed, and cut into ¼-inch-thick slices

½ teaspoon minced garlic

1 teaspoon peeled, grated fresh ginger

1 carrot, peeled and cut crosswise into ¼-inch-thick slices

¾ cup low-sodium chicken stock

1 tablespoon all-purpose flour

1 tablespoon low-sodium tamari sauce

Zest and juice of 1 lemon

1 cup green beans, cut into 2-inch pieces

PER SERVING

Calories: 216
Fat: 4.4g
Saturated fat: 1.6g
Protein: 28.5g
Carbohydrates: 14.5g
Sodium: 417mg
Fiber: 4.0g
Sugar: 5.1g

Chicken Pineapple Salad Pockets

The combination of pineapple and chicken is somehow perfect on the palate, and mixing in the crunch of almonds lifts this dish to the sublime. Fresh pineapple is the best option, but canned pineapple packed in 100 percent pineapple juice is acceptable in a pinch. Keep in mind that the canning process usually destroys most natural vitamin C in fruit, and in the case of pineapple, an anti-inflammatory enzyme called bromelain is also eliminated.

1 cup diced cooked chicken breast

½ cup diced pineapple, fresh or canned

½ cup diced cucumber

¼ cup shredded carrot

1 scallion, white and green parts, chopped

3 tablespoons fat-free plain yogurt

2 tablespoons slivered almonds

Pinch sea salt

Pinch freshly ground black pepper

1 cup shredded lettuce

2 (6-inch) whole-wheat pitas, halved

1. In a large bowl, mix the chicken, pineapple, cucumber, carrot, scallion, yogurt, almonds, salt, and pepper until well combined.

2. Divide the lettuce evenly between the 4 pita halves.

3. Spoon the chicken mixture into the pita halves and serve 2 halves per person.

TIP: *Making this tempting sandwich dairy-free is as easy as swapping the Greek yogurt with a soy, rice, or coconut yogurt substitute. Vanilla yogurt (either milk-based or vegan) is also a nice choice for a little extra flavor.*

PAIR WITH . . . Velvety Chocolate Pudding (page 202)

PER SERVING
Calories: 392
Fat: 7.4g
Saturated fat: 0.0g
Protein: 33.6g
Carbohydrates: 50.6g
Sodium: 577g
Fiber: 7.1g
Sugar: 11.9g

Chicken Florentine Casserole

Casseroles are one of the most comforting dishes in the culinary world, which is probably why they are an immediate choice for a housewarming gift or a drop-off gift for people in hard times. "Casserole" refers to the dish that the food is cooked in rather than the combination of tempting ingredients. This casserole is cheesy, slightly chewy from the brown rice, and studded with juicy chunks of chicken and earthy spinach. You might want to break out the old-fashioned TV trays, cover up your knees with a blanket for two, and enjoy your chicken Florentine elbow to elbow on the couch.

1. Preheat the oven to 350°F.

2. Heat the olive oil in a medium skillet over medium-high heat. Sauté the onion, mushrooms, carrot, and garlic until softened, about 5 minutes. Stir in the flour until it looks pasty, about 1 minute. Stir in the milk and continue stirring until the sauce thickens, about 4 minutes. Add the cheese and nutmeg. Season with pepper.

3. Put the chicken, rice, and spinach in a large bowl, pour the sauce over, and mix well with a large spoon.

4. Spoon the chicken mixture into an 8-by-8-inch casserole dish. Bake until bubbly and lightly browned, about 15 minutes.

TIP: *Cooked brown rice can be refrigerated for up to four days as long as you cool it quickly and store it in a shallow sealed container. Make a big batch at the beginning of the week to use for speedy salads, side dishes, and casseroles.*

PAIR WITH . . . Chunky Applesauce (page 201)

1 tablespoon olive oil
1 onion, chopped
½ cup sliced button mushrooms
½ cup shredded carrot
1 teaspoon minced garlic
1 tablespoon all-purpose flour
1 cup skim milk
¼ cup grated Parmesan cheese
Pinch ground nutmeg
Freshly ground black pepper
1 (6-ounce) cooked skinless, boneless chicken breast, shredded
2 cups cooked brown rice
2 cups packed fresh spinach

PER SERVING
Calories: 565
Fat: 18.0g
Saturated fat: 4.8g
Protein: 39.5g
Carbohydrates: 60.2g
Sodium: 312mg
Fiber: 3.9g
Sugar: 9.3g

Chicken Cacciatore

PREP TIME
10 MINUTES

COOK TIME
45 MINUTES

In the interest of a faster cooking time, you will be using chunks of chicken breast in this recipe rather than a full breast or the more traditional legs and thighs. Many cacciatore recipes require several hours on the stove or in the oven to get the cuts of poultry cooked through and tender. If you want to try this recipe on the weekend, when you might have a little more time, use chicken thighs: dark chicken meat has much more flavor than the leaner breasts.

¼ cup all-purpose flour

Pinch sea salt

Pinch freshly ground black pepper

1 teaspoon olive oil

2 (6-ounce) chicken breasts cut into 2-inch chunks

2 carrots, peeled and cut into ½-inch pieces

1 celery stalk, chopped

1 sweet onion, chopped

1 tablespoon minced garlic

2 tablespoons tomato paste

½ cup reduced-sodium chicken stock

½ cup dry red wine

1 large tomato, chopped

1 teaspoon chopped fresh oregano, or ½ teaspoon dried oregano

1 teaspoon chopped fresh basil, or ½ teaspoon dried basil

½ teaspoon chopped fresh thyme, or ¼ teaspoon dried thyme

Pinch red pepper flakes

1. In a small bowl, stir together the flour, salt, and pepper.

2. Heat the olive oil in a large skillet over medium-high heat.

3. While the oil heats, dredge the chicken pieces in the flour, shaking off the excess. Cook the chicken for about 6 minutes, until browned on all sides; then remove with a slotted spoon to a plate.

4. Add the carrots, celery, onion, and garlic to the skillet and sauté until softened, about 4 minutes. Stir in the tomato paste, chicken stock, wine, tomato, oregano, basil, thyme, and red pepper flakes. Bring to a boil and return the chicken to the skillet. Reduce the heat to low and simmer, covered, until the chicken is tender, about 30 minutes.

TIP: *Cacciatore is a wonderful rustic dish to make when you have special company over for dinner. Doubling and tripling this recipe is as simple as multiplying the ingredients by the number you need, except for the chili flakes. Add the chili flakes at the end in tiny pinches until you achieve the desired heat.*

PAIR WITH . . . Herbed Egg Noodles (page 192)

PER SERVING
Calories: 519
Fat: 19.3g
Saturated fat: 4.0g
Protein: 54.4g
Carbohydrates: 27.5g
Sodium: 361mg
Fiber: 4.9g
Sugar: 8.9g

Sesame Chicken Meatballs

If you have ever looked for an Asian-themed healthy version of a meatball sandwich, your quest is over. Sesame seeds and rich tamari sauce provide just a hint of exotic flair, and the easy execution of the meatballs could mean you will make them a weekly addition to your meals. You might want to triple this recipe and freeze individual portions of meatballs in resealable baggies for a quick snack or lunch choice. Simply thaw the meatballs in the refrigerator overnight and enjoy them the next day with no loss of texture or taste.

1. In a large bowl, thoroughly mix the chicken, bread crumbs, sesame seeds, egg white, and tamari and season with pepper. Form the chicken mixture into eight meatballs.

2. Heat the olive oil in a large skillet over medium heat. Cook the meatballs until they are cooked through and browned on all sides, about 8 minutes. Remove from the heat.

3. Stuff each pita half with two meatballs. Top the meatballs with the shredded cucumber, sour cream, and scallion.

TIP: *This recipe could also be made with ground pork or turkey instead of the chicken with fabulous results.*

PAIR WITH . . . Maple Pecan Tapioca Pudding (page 202)

10 ounces lean ground chicken

1 teaspoon seasoned whole-wheat bread crumbs

1 teaspoon toasted sesame seeds

1 egg white

1 teaspoon low-sodium tamari sauce

Freshly ground black pepper

1 teaspoon olive oil

2 whole-wheat pitas, halved

½ cup shredded cucumber, with the liquid squeezed out

2 tablespoons fat-free sour cream

½ scallion, white and green parts, cut diagonally into ⅛-inch-thick slices

PER SERVING

Calories: 419
Fat: 12.4g
Saturated fat: 3.2g
Protein: 38.0g
Carbohydrates: 40.3g
Sodium: 560mg
Fiber: 5.2g
Sugar: 1.8g

Paprika Chicken

GLUTEN-FREE
DAIRY-FREE
MAKE AHEAD
30 MINUTES
ONE-POT

PREP TIME
5 MINUTES

COOK TIME
16 MINUTES

There is a famous Hungarian dish called goulash that pairs paprika and chicken together in a tangy sour cream sauce. This recipe is the stripped-down version of that artery-clogging stew. Lean skinless chicken breasts are rubbed with paprika and pan-seared to a tempting golden brown. There is no rich sauce, but that omission allows the taste of the poultry and spice to shine through unimpeded.

1 teaspoon olive oil

2 (6-ounce) boneless, skinless chicken breasts

½ teaspoon paprika

1 teaspoon ground cumin

Sea salt

Freshly ground black pepper

PER SERVING
Calories: 349
Fat: 15.2g
Saturated fat: 3.8g
Protein: 49.5g
Carbohydrates: 0.8g
Sodium: 265mg
Fiber: 0.0g
Sugar: 0.0g

1. Heat the olive oil in a medium skillet over medium-high heat.

2. Season the chicken breasts evenly with the paprika, cumin, salt, and pepper.

3. Cook the chicken breasts until they are golden brown and cooked through, about 8 minutes per side. Remove from the heat and let stand for 5 minutes before slicing each breast into 3 pieces. Serve.

TIP: *Paprika is made from finely grinding dried chile and sweet red bell peppers into a powder. This piquant spice imparts a lovely color and flavor to ingredients and some health benefits as well. Paprika can help lower blood pressure, promote healthy digestion, and help protect the eyes from macular degeneration associated with aging.*

PAIR WITH . . . Cinnamon Couscous (page 193)

DAIRY-FREE
MAKE AHEAD
30 MINUTES
ONE-POT

PREP TIME
10 MINUTES
(+ chilling time)

COOK TIME
15 MINUTES

Curried Chicken Couscous

You might think of North African bazaars when this fragrant concoction is placed on your table. The melding of curry, lemony cumin, and warm allspice creates a dish equally tempting to the eyes and nose. The dried cranberries are a North American addition; apricots or dates are a more traditional dried fruit used in this dish. The cranberries are like pretty jewels in the fluffy couscous, and they provide interesting tart bursts of flavor in each spoonful.

1. Heat the olive oil in a large saucepan over medium-low heat. Sauté the scallion and bell pepper until softened, about 3 minutes. Stir in the chicken stock and bring to a boil.

2. Remove the saucepan from the heat. Stir in the couscous, salt, curry powder, cumin, allspice, and raisins. Cover the saucepan and let sit for 10 minutes.

3. Fluff the cooked couscous with a fork. Add the chicken and cashews and mix well. Refrigerate for about 1 hour, fluff with a fork, and serve.

TIP: *Cashews are not nuts; they are the seeds found on the bottom of the cashew apple. They are packed with heart-healthy monounsaturated fats and contain almost 100 percent of the recommended daily amount of copper. Copper is essential for strong bones and can help lower cholesterol while reducing the risk of osteoporosis.*

PAIR WITH . . . Pecan Honey Bananas (page 200)

1 teaspoon olive oil

1 scallion, white and green parts, cut into ¼-inch-thick slices

1 red bell pepper, seeded, deribbed, and diced

1 cup low-sodium chicken stock

¾ cup uncooked whole-wheat couscous

Pinch sea salt

1 teaspoon good-quality curry powder

¼ teaspoon ground cumin

Pinch ground allspice

½ cup golden raisins

1 (6-ounce) cooked skinless, boneless chicken breast, cut into ½-inch chunks

1 tablespoon chopped cashews

PER SERVING
Calories: 560
Fat: 8.3g
Saturated fat: 0.9g
Protein: 39.1g
Carbohydrates: 83.9g
Sodium: 285mg
Fiber: 6.1g
Sugar: 23.4g

Roasted Chicken with Yogurt Sauce

Cool cucumber-flecked yogurt sauce spooned over a spiced juicy chicken breast is like a refreshing breeze that lifts the lingering heat of summer at the end of a sunny day. Hot paprika contains capsaicin, which is the compound that creates the heat in chiles. If you are a fan of spicy food, use smoked hot paprika for a truly pleasing depth and layering of flavor. Smoked paprika is usually Spanish in origin and is made from dried chiles that are smoked over oak.

PREP TIME
10 MINUTES

COOK TIME
20 MINUTES

1 medium cucumber

¼ scallion, white and green parts, chopped

2 tablespoons fat-free vanilla yogurt

Juice of ½ lime

½ teaspoon lime zest

Pinch sea salt

Pinch freshly ground black pepper

Nonstick cooking spray

2 (6-ounce) skinless, boneless chicken breasts

1 teaspoon chopped fresh thyme, or ½ teaspoon dried thyme

Dash hot or smoked paprika

PER SERVING
Calories: 233
Fat: 6.2g
Saturated fat: 2.3g
Protein: 38.9g
Carbohydrates: 4.4g
Sodium: 188mg
Fiber: 0.6g
Sugar: 1.7g

1. Preheat the oven to 400°F.

2. Grate cucumber into a colander and squeeze to release liquid. In a small bowl combine the cucumber, scallion, yogurt, and lime juice and zest. Season with salt and pepper and set aside.

3. Place a small skillet over medium-high heat and spray lightly with the cooking spray. Season the chicken with thyme, paprika, and pepper. Cook the chicken on both sides until lightly browned, about 2 minutes per side.

4. Transfer the chicken to a baking pan and roast in the oven until cooked through, about 15 minutes. Serve with the yogurt sauce.

TIP: *The roasted chicken in this recipe is juicy and flavorful, so double the recipe and cook a few extra breasts to use later in the week for salads, sandwiches, and soups. Cool the chicken down quickly in the refrigerator, and store it in a sealed container or a resealable plastic bag for up to three days.*

PAIR WITH . . . Honey- and Herb-Glazed Carrots (page 188)

Turkey Meat Loaf

Meat loaf is a homey, nutritious, old-fashioned entrée that can be thrown together in about five minutes and popped in the oven to cook while you make the accompanying dishes. You might be more familiar with ground beef or ground pork meat loaf recipes, which tend to be oily enough to require tipping out the excess grease from the loaf pan after it is cooked. Extra-lean turkey can be up to 99 percent lean, which means no fatty residue but a somehow very similar taste.

1. Heat the oven to 450°F.

2. In a large bowl, mix all the ingredients together until well combined. Press the turkey mixture into a loaf in a baking dish.

3. Place the baking dish on a baking sheet and bake until the meat loaf is cooked through, about 30 minutes. Remove from the oven and let sit for about 10 minutes before serving.

TIP: *Leftover cold turkey meat loaf is one of the best fillings for your sandwich the next day. It is particularly tasty with a generous splash of hot sauce.*

PAIR WITH . . . Creamy Mashed Cauliflower (page 189)

¾ pound extra-lean ground turkey

2 tablespoons whole-wheat bread crumbs

1 egg white

¼ cup grated sweet onion

¼ cup skim milk

1 tablespoon chopped fresh parsley, or 1 teaspoon dried parsley

Pinch sea salt

Pinch freshly ground black pepper

PER SERVING
Calories: 311
Fat: 12.5g
Saturated fat: 3.9g
Protein: 35.7g
Carbohydrates: 7.9g
Sodium: 332mg
Fiber: 0.6g
Sugar: 2.7g

Turkey Bolognese

GLUTEN-FREE
DAIRY-FREE
MAKE AHEAD
ONE-POT

PREP TIME
5 MINUTES

COOK TIME
35 MINUTES

Bolognese sauce originates in Bologna, Italy, and is usually a meaty sauce that is cooked very slowly on the back burner of the stove, often all day. This variation uses turkey, and is not a true Bolognese, because it is cooked rather quickly in comparison to the slow-cooked original. However, there is a richness to the sauce that hints at it having spent hours maturing in the pot over a low flame.

½ **pound extra-lean ground turkey**

½ **sweet onion, chopped**

1 **teaspoon minced garlic**

1 **celery stalk, diced**

5 **sun-dried tomatoes, chopped**

1 **(28-ounce) can sodium-free diced tomatoes**

¼ **cup low-sodium chicken stock**

2 **tablespoons chopped fresh basil, or 1 tablespoon dried basil**

Pinch red pepper flakes

PER SERVING
Calories: 280
Fat: 8.3g
Saturated fat: 2.5g
Protein: 22.6g
Carbohydrates: 5.3g
Sodium: 267mg
Fiber: 1.2g
Sugar: 2.8g

1. Place a large skillet over medium-high heat, and cook the ground turkey until it is cooked through and browned, about 6 minutes. Add the onion, garlic, and celery, and sauté until the vegetables are softened, about 3 minutes.

2. Stir in the sun-dried tomatoes, diced tomatoes, and chicken stock. Bring to a boil; then reduce the heat to low and simmer for about 25 minutes.

3. Serve over your favorite pasta, topped with the basil and red pepper flakes.

TIP: *Turkey is considered to be a healthy protein choice, but it is much higher in sodium than other meats, almost double in some comparisons. If you have an issue with high blood pressure, keep an eye on your sodium consumption.*

PAIR WITH . . . Herbed Egg Noodles (page 192)

PREP TIME
30 MINUTES
(+ chilling time)

Chili Turkey Vermicelli Salad

Some foods, such as chateaubriand or coq au vin, seem very serious in nature, demanding elegant folded napkins and heavy silverware. Then there are foods that seem joyful and casual, meant to be eaten in a park or campsite, and this salad is one of those dishes. It bursts with multiple fresh colors and interesting textures swathed in strong exotic flavors. The best part of this salad, besides eating it, is that you can make a double batch because the leftovers taste even better the next day. This salad is best made with fresh mint.

1. Soak the rice noodles according to the package instructions. (This can be done overnight.) Drain and set aside.

2. Combine the lime juice and zest, honey, tamari, chile, ginger, and garlic in a small bowl, and set aside.

3. In a large bowl, toss the remaining ingredients together; then stir in the rice noodles and dressing. Refrigerate for at least 4 hours to let the flavors mellow. Serve chilled.

TIP: *Jicama is a root vegetable that looks a little like a potato. Its thick light brown skin encases crisp snowy flesh that tastes a little like a starchy Asian pear. Leftover jicama can be juiced, shredded for slaws and salsas, or eaten in juicy chunks as a snack.*

PAIR WITH . . . Mixed Berries with Orange Cream (page 198)

½ package (100 grams) rice vermicelli noodles

Juice and zest of 2 limes

1 tablespoon honey

1 teaspoon low-sodium tamari sauce

1 chile, finely chopped

1 teaspoon peeled, grated fresh ginger

½ teaspoon minced garlic

1 cup shredded cooked turkey breast

1 carrot, peeled and julienned

1 cup julienned jicama

1 red bell pepper, seeded, deribbed, and julienned

2 tablespoons chopped fresh coriander

2 tablespoons chopped fresh mint or 1 tablespoon dried mint

1 tablespoon chopped roasted peanuts

PER SERVING
Calories: 338
Fat: 3.8g
Saturated fat: 0.7g
Protein: 17.2g
Carbohydrates: 59.0g
Sodium: 932mg
Fiber: 12.3g
Sugar: 20.0g

Ginger Turkey Rissoles

This dish comes together quite quickly once you get the hang of breading your turkey mixture. You can complete the rissoles from bowl to plate in under 30 minutes with practice. If you are not in too much of a hurry, one of the best ways to ensure your rissoles have a uniform shape and stay together during the cooking process is to chill them for 30 minutes after rolling them in the bread crumbs. You can even make them the day before and store them in a container in the refrigerator until you want to cook them.

PREP TIME
10 MINUTES

COOK TIME
30 MINUTES

8 ounces extra-lean
    ground turkey
1 scallion, white and green
    parts, finely chopped
1 teaspoon minced garlic
1 cup grated zucchini
¼ cup frozen peas
¼ cup whole-wheat
    bread crumbs
1 teaspoon olive oil

PER SERVING
Calories: 276
Fat: 12.3g
Saturated fat: 2.5g
Protein: 27.6g
Carbohydrates: 16.2g
Sodium: 206mg
Fiber: 3.0g
Sugar: 3.1g

1. Preheat the oven to 350°F. Line a baking sheet with aluminum foil.

2. Combine the ground turkey, scallion, garlic, zucchini, and peas together in a medium bowl. Put the bread crumbs in a small shallow bowl. Shape the turkey mixture into 4 patties and coat evenly with the bread crumbs.

3. Heat the olive oil in a medium skillet over medium-high heat. Brown the rissoles on all sides until uniformly golden, about 10 minutes in total.

4. Transfer the rissoles to the prepared baking sheet. Bake them until cooked through, turning them once, about 20 minutes.

TIP: *Rissoles are also called croquettes and are a popular food in many countries such as Indonesia, Australia, and Portugal. This recipe could be converted to a vegetarian dish by using ground chickpeas instead of turkey, although you might have to add an egg to moisten the mixture enough to stay together.*

PAIR WITH . . . Spring Vegetable Ragout (page 190)

PREP TIME
15 MINUTES
(+ chilling time)

Asian Duck Coleslaw

Duck and Asian flavors are a natural pairing because both have strong flavors that do not overpower each other. This recipe lifts unpretentious coleslaw to a higher level, creating something truly special. Pistachios would make a nice garnish if peanut allergies are an issue in your home.

1. In a small bowl, stir together the tamari, sesame oil, ginger, chile, and honey until well blended.

2. In a large bowl, toss together the remaining ingredients until well mixed. Add the dressing and toss until well coated.

3. Serve immediately or refrigerate the coleslaw until you are ready to eat.

TIP: *Don't be surprised at the amount of fat that renders from the duck breast in this recipe when you roast it in advance. One of the reasons this meat is so tender and flavorful is this profusion of fat. Score the duck skin with a knife and roast the breast skin-side-down in a 350°F oven for about 15 minutes to get a juicy finished product. And if you're a fan of French cooking, you can reserve the rendered fat to use in traditional recipes.*

PAIR WITH . . . Nutmeg-Baked Peaches (page 199)

1 teaspoon low-sodium
    tamari sauce
2 tablespoons sesame oil
1 teaspoon peeled, grated
    fresh ginger
½ red chile, seeded
    and chopped
1 teaspoon honey
1 cup shredded white cabbage
1 cup shredded carrots
½ cup bean sprouts
2 scallions, white and green
    parts, cut diagonally into
    ⅛-inch-thick slices
¼ cup chopped cilantro
1 (8-ounce) cooked duck
    breast, shredded
2 teaspoons chopped peanuts

PER SERVING
Calories: 357
Fat: 20.1g
Saturated fat: 2.2g
Protein: 30.0g
Carbohydrates: 14.9g
Sodium: 401mg
Fiber: 3.3g
Sugar: 7.6g

Berry-Marinated Duck Breasts

GLUTEN-FREE
DAIRY-FREE
30 MINUTES
ONE-POT

PREP TIME
10 MINUTES

COOK TIME
20 MINUTES

Fruit is often used as a tenderizing marinade for meats because it has a natural acid content. In this recipe, the duck is melt-in-your-mouth tender without spending hours marinating in the refrigerator, so the sauce can be made fresh and spooned on at the end. Purchase premade raspberry vinegar or create your own infusion by simply placing fresh berries in a glass jar and filling it to the top with white wine vinegar. Store the jar in a cool place out of direct sunlight for a few weeks and then strain the berries out. Note that homemade vinegar can be stronger than store bought, depending on the amount of berries you use and the length of time you allow the mixture to sit.

1 teaspoon olive oil

2 (6-ounce) skinless duck breasts, trimmed of visible fat

Sea salt

Freshly ground black pepper

¼ cup raspberry vinegar

½ teaspoon minced garlic

½ cup red wine

2 tablespoons honey

1 cup fresh raspberries

PER SERVING
Calories: 392
Fat: 9.5g
Saturated fat: 0.0g
Protein: 38.3g
Carbohydrates: 26.8g
Sodium: 123mg
Fiber: 4.1g
Sugar: 20.6g

1. Heat the olive oil in a medium skillet over medium-high heat.

2. Season the duck breasts lightly with salt and pepper. Put the duck in the skillet and cook until they are golden brown and cooked to the desired doneness, about 6 minutes per side for medium. Transfer the duck breasts to a plate and cover loosely with aluminum foil to keep warm.

3. Pour out any excess fat from the skillet and return the pan to the heat. Add the vinegar, garlic, and wine and cook for 3 minutes, or until reduced by about half. Stir in the honey and cook for 1 more minute. Stir in the raspberries, breaking some up with the back of a spoon.

4. Cut each duck breast into 4 slices and serve topped with the raspberry sauce.

TIP: *Blueberries are also a tasty option for this sauce because duck combines well with almost any fruit. If you want to try blueberries, you can keep the raspberry vinegar in the recipe or use balsamic vinegar instead.*

PAIR WITH . . . Roasted Root Vegetables (page 191)

Spice-Rubbed Duck Breast with Pear and Hazelnut

PREP TIME
10 MINUTES

COOK TIME
15 MINUTES
(+ resting time)

The flavors of juicy sweet pear, crunchy hazelnuts, and rich duck merge together in this gorgeous dish, making it an ideal choice for a romantic meal for two. If you leave the skin on the duck for the cooking process, make sure you score it with a sharp knife so the fat can render out. Rub the spice mix under the skin at least partway, because it is healthier to remove the duck skin before eating this dish and you don't want to throw away any of the flavor.

1. Preheat the oven to 350°F.

2. In a small bowl, mix together the paprika, chili powder, cinnamon, and coriander.

3. Place the duck breasts on a plate and rub the spice mixture into both sides to coat.

4. Heat the olive oil in a large skillet over medium-high heat. Sear the duck breasts on both sides, until lightly browned, about 3 minutes per side. Transfer the skillet to the oven and roast the duck to the desired doneness, about 8 minutes for medium. Remove the duck breasts from the oven and let them rest on a cutting board for at least 10 minutes.

5. Thickly slice the breasts and arrange them on top of the pear slices. Garnish the duck with the hazelnuts and thyme.

TIP: *There might be spice rub left over after you make this recipe, depending on the size of the duck breasts. The mixture works well with pork and chicken as well, so transfer the rub to a resealable bag or a small airtight jar, and store out of direct sunlight.*

PAIR WITH . . . Mashed Roasted Butternut Squash (page 192)

1 teaspoon sweet paprika
½ teaspoon chili powder
¼ teaspoon ground cinnamon
¼ teaspoon ground coriander
2 (6-ounce) skinless duck breasts, trimmed of visible fat
1 teaspoon olive oil
1 pear, cored and cut lengthwise into ⅛-inch-thick slices
2 tablespoons chopped hazelnuts
1 tablespoon chopped fresh thyme or 1 teaspoon dried thyme

PER SERVING
Calories: 316
Fat: 12.3g
Saturated fat: 0.6g
Protein: 38.7g
Carbohydrates: 13.0g
Sodium: 8mg
Fiber: 3.5g
Sugar: 7.2g

Beef, Pork, and Lamb

Flank Steak with Caramelized Onions

PREP TIME
10 MINUTES

COOK TIME
30 MINUTES
(+ resting time)

For a festive family-style (one-plate) meal, you can heap the sliced flank steak on a platter surrounded by the onions and peppers. Heap salsa, fat-free sour cream, shredded lettuce, and shredded low-fat cheese in pretty decorative bowls and arrange the bowls around the platter. After all that bounty is on your table, all you need is a stack of warm tortillas and a pitcher of sangria for an intimate fajita fiesta.

1. Heat the olive oil in a large skillet over medium-high heat. Sauté the onions for about 2 minutes to coat with oil, and then reduce the heat to low. Cover and cook, stirring occasionally, until softened, about 8 minutes. Stir in the bell pepper, basil, and oregano; cook, uncovered, until the onions are golden and the peppers softened, about 4 minutes. Cover and remove the skillet from the heat.

2. Season the steak on both sides with salt and pepper.

3. Preheat a grill to medium-high.

4. Grill the steak for 4 to 6 minutes per side for medium, turning once. Transfer the steak from the grill to a cutting board, and let rest for 10 minutes.

5. Cut the steak diagonally across the grain into thin slices. Serve topped with the onion mixture.

TIP: *Although the opinions of chefs differ, some of the best onions to caramelize are Vidalia onions. These sweet beauties have a higher sugar content, which means it takes less time to get a golden hue and the finished onion has a richer taste. Walla Walla Sweets make a perfect substitute. If you do not have a barbecue, place a large skillet over medium high heat and pan sear the flank steak about six minutes per side for medium-rare.*

PAIR WITH . . . Grilled Asparagus (page 188)

1 teaspoon olive oil

1 sweet onion, thinly sliced

1 red bell pepper, seeded, deribbed, and cut into thin strips

1 teaspoon chopped fresh basil or ½ teaspoon dried basil

1 teaspoon chopped fresh oregano or ½ teaspoon dried oregano

1 (8-ounce) beef flank steak, trimmed of visible fat

Sea salt

Freshly ground black pepper

PER SERVING
Calories: 267
Fat: 9.6g
Saturated fat: 3.0g
Protein: 35.4g
Carbohydrates: 9.5g
Sodium: 193mg
Fiber: 2.6g
Sugar: 4.8g

Maple-Marinated Flank Steak

GLUTEN-FREE
DAIRY-FREE
30 MINUTES

PREP TIME
5 MINUTES

COOK TIME
16 MINUTES

The combination of a mustard-spiked maple glaze and the juices from your grilled steak collecting on your plate will have you reaching for a piece of fresh bread to sop everything up. The sweet, almost smoky marinade is a perfect foil for beef, but would also be delectable with pork. If you don't have a grill, this steak can be cooked in a large skillet over medium-high heat, about five minutes per side for medium doneness.

1 tablespoon pure maple syrup
1 tablespoon freshly squeezed
   lemon juice
½ teaspoon grainy mustard
1 teaspoon minced garlic
½ pound flank steak
Sea salt
Freshly ground black pepper

PER SERVING
Calories: 263
Fat: 11.5g
Saturated fat: 4.4g
Protein: 30.4g
Carbohydrates: 7.4g
Sodium: 212mg
Fiber: 0.0g
Sugar: 6.1g

1. Combine the maple syrup, lemon juice, mustard, and garlic in a small saucepan. Place the saucepan over medium heat and bring to a boil. Reduce the heat to low and let the sauce simmer for 1 minute. Remove from the heat and set aside.

2. Season the steak lightly with salt and pepper.

3. Preheat a grill to medium-high.

4. Grill the steak until it reaches your desired doneness, 4 to 6 minutes per side for medium. Remove to a cutting board and let rest for 10 minutes. Slice it thinly on a diagonal across the grain. Serve drizzled with the sauce.

TIP: *Maple syrup is considered to be a healthy alternative to refined sugars in baking and other types of recipes. It is also a good source of iron, potassium, and calcium. If your local natural food market carries it, try thicker Grade B maple syrup, which is generally cheaper and more flavorful than the very expensive Grade A.*

PAIR WITH . . . Creamy Mashed Cauliflower (page 189)

Beef Tomato Ragù

The enticing aroma of fresh herbs, tomatoes, and pungent garlic will waft through your house as this ragù simmers slowly on the stove. Traditional ragùs are cooked slowly, but they do freeze beautifully if you want to cook a double batch on your day off or on the weekend. When the ragù is ready, cool it down quickly in the refrigerator. When it is completely chilled, transfer it to containers or resealable plastic freezer bags.

1. Heat the olive oil in a large saucepan over medium-high heat. Brown the beef chunks on all sides, about 5 minutes. Transfer the beef to a plate with a slotted spoon.

2. Add the shallots, garlic, carrot, and celery to the saucepan and sauté for 4 minutes. Stir in the thyme, rosemary, and wine. Simmer until the wine is reduced by half, about 2 minutes.

3. Add the beef, accumulated juices from the plate, tomato paste, tomato, beef stock, and water.

4. Bring to a boil, stirring; then reduce the heat to low. Cover and simmer the sauce until the beef is tender, about 1½ hours. Season with salt and pepper.

TIP: *This recipe can also be made in a slow cooker, so it is waiting, hot and fragrant, when you get home from work. In the morning, simply brown the beef chunks and then pile all the ingredients in your slow cooker, stirring to combine well. Set it for the appropriate time and forget about it until the mouthwatering aroma greets you at the door.*

PAIR WITH . . . Herbed Egg Noodles (page 192)

1 tablespoon olive oil

10 ounces beef chuck steak, cut into 1-inch chunks

2 shallots, peeled and quartered

1 teaspoon minced garlic

1 carrot, peeled and cut into ½-inch pieces

1 celery stalk, cut into ¼-inch-thick slices

1 tablespoon chopped fresh thyme, or 1 teaspoon dried thyme

½ teaspoon chopped fresh rosemary, or ¼ teaspoon dried rosemary

¼ cup dry red wine

1 teaspoon tomato paste

1 tomato, diced

½ cup low-sodium beef stock

½ cup water

Sea salt

Freshly ground black pepper

PER SERVING
Calories: 376
Fat: 16.0g
Saturated fat: 4.4g
Protein: 44.4g
Carbohydrates: 6.6g
Sodium: 157mg
Fiber: 1.8g
Sugar: 3.0g

Beef and Cabbage Stir-Fry

GLUTEN-FREE
DAIRY-FREE
30 MINUTES

PREP TIME
15 MINUTES

COOK TIME
15 MINUTES

The cabbage in this recipe acts like noodles in a chow mein or pad thai because they soak up the piquant peanut sauce and provide bulk to the dish. Cabbage has a stronger flavor than neutral noodles, adding another layer to the delicious taste profile. You can use either smooth or chunky peanut butter in your sauce, depending on your preference or what is in your cupboard. For peanut-free households, try substituting tahini (sesame paste) or miso (fermented soy paste). And of course, always read labels to reduce risk of cross-contamination.

2 tablespoons natural
   peanut butter

Juice of 1 orange

1 teaspoon rice vinegar

1 teaspoon low-sodium
   tamari sauce

1 teaspoon honey

2 teaspoons olive oil, divided

¼ sweet onion, cut into
   ¼-inch-thick slices

1 teaspoon minced garlic

10 ounces sirloin steak,
   trimmed of fat and cut into
   ¼-inch-thick slices

⅓ head Savoy cabbage, cut
   into ¼-inch-thick slices

2 tablespoons water

2 carrots, peeled and grated

PER SERVING
Calories: 515
Fat: 24.1g
Saturated fat: 5.9g
Protein: 51.4g
Carbohydrates: 22.2g
Sodium: 509mg
Fiber: 5.2g
Sugar: 12.9g

1. In a small bowl, stir together the peanut butter, orange juice, vinegar, tamari sauce, and honey until well combined. Set aside.

2. Heat 1 teaspoon of the olive oil in a large skillet over medium heat. Sauté the garlic until fragrant, about 2 minutes. Add the beef slices to the skillet and sauté until browned, about 3 minutes. Transfer the beef mixture to a bowl and set aside.

3. Sauté the cabbage in the remaining 1 teaspoon olive oil and the water until the cabbage starts to wilt, about 5 minutes. Stir in the carrots and sauté until softened, about 3 minutes. Add the beef and juices in the bowl back to the skillet, add the sauce, and stir to combine. Sauté for 1 minute more and serve.

TIP: *Turn any leftover cabbage into creamy coleslaw, or try your hand at making tangy sauerkraut. The large outer leaves of this cruciferous vegetable also can be wrapped around tasty beef filling to make traditional cabbage rolls.*

PAIR WITH . . . Broccoli with Lemon Butter (page 188)

Spicy Beef Tagine

As discussed previously on page 59, a tagine is actually a clay cooking vessel used in some North African countries, and the name has become synonymous for this very unique style of cuisine. Classic tagine recipes often take hours and hours to make because the cooking vessel is designed to cook food slowly, keeping in all the moisture. This recipe is quite speedy for a tagine because it calls for ground beef instead of beef chunks. The aroma of the exotic spices of this dish will draw you to the table. Although garam masala is a traditional North Indian spice, it works well in this Moroccan-style dish.

1. Place a large saucepan over medium-high heat. Cook the beef, stirring and breaking up any large chunks, until it is cooked through, about 7 minutes. Transfer the beef to a bowl with a slotted spoon and set aside.

2. Add the olive oil and sauté the eggplant for 5 minutes. Stir in the zucchini, garlic, ginger, garam masala, and cinnamon, and sauté for 2 minutes. Add the tomato, olives, and chickpeas, and return the beef and any juice in the bowl to the saucepan.

3. Bring the tagine to a boil; then reduce the heat to low and simmer, covered, until the eggplant is tender, about 12 minutes. Remove from the heat and stir in the chili paste.

TIP: *Cut any leftover eggplant into chunks, toss them with a little olive oil, and bake them in the oven at 350°F for 30 minutes. Purée the roasted eggplant with garlic, onions, and tahini to make baba ghanoush, a delicious Middle East-style dip and spread.*

PAIR WITH . . . Fresh Gingered Melon (page 198)

6 ounces extra-lean ground beef

1 teaspoon olive oil

½ small eggplant, peeled and cut into 1-inch chunks

1 zucchini, cut into ½-inch rounds

2 teaspoons minced garlic

1 teaspoon peeled, grated fresh ginger

½ teaspoon garam masala

Dash ground cinnamon

1 tomato, diced

2 tablespoons pitted black olives, halved

1 cup sodium-free canned chickpeas, rinsed and drained

1 teaspoon chili paste

PER SERVING
Calories: 328
Fat: 10.9g
Saturated fat: 3.2g
Protein: 31.6g
Carbohydrates: 27.5g
Sodium: 182mg
Fiber: 10.8g
Sugar: 6.3g

Gourmet Sloppy Joes

DAIRY-FREE

MAKE AHEAD

30 MINUTES

If you have a food processor or blender, your preparation time for the chopped vegetables in this dish will be considerably faster than if you have to chop everything by hand. If you want to chop using a manual method, make sure you produce a very fine dice of everything, especially the onion, to get consistency in the flavor of the dish.

PREP TIME
10 MINUTES

COOK TIME
20 MINUTES

½ carrot, peeled
¼ sweet onion
3 button mushrooms
1 garlic clove
4 ounces lean ground beef
½ teaspoon red wine vinegar
Dash Worcestershire sauce
½ cup low-sodium
     tomato sauce
½ teaspoon tomato paste
2 Kaiser rolls, cut in half

PER SERVING
Calories: 296
Fat: 7.1g
Saturated fat: 2.2g
Protein: 19.1g
Carbohydrates: 36.2g
Sodium: 373mg
Fiber: 2.4g
Sugar: 6.2g

1. Place the carrot, onion, mushrooms, and garlic in a blender and pulse until finely chopped. Set aside.

2. In a medium skillet over medium-high heat, brown the beef, cooking thoroughly, for about 6 minutes. Add the vegetables and cook, stirring, for 4 minutes. Stir in the vinegar, Worcestershire sauce, tomato sauce, and tomato paste. Cover and reduce the heat to low. Simmer the mixture for 5 minutes.

3. Meanwhile, preheat the oven to broil. Toast the rolls cut-side up under the broiler for 1 minute, watching carefully so they don't burn.

4. Divide the Sloppy Joe mixture between the two rolls and serve.

TIP: *Spoon the extra tomato sauce into a clean ice cube tray and freeze the sauce, covered, for three or four months. Add the cubes whole and frozen to simmering sauces and soups when you need a little extra tomato flavor.*

PAIR WITH . . . Speedy Strawberry Ice Cream (page 198)

Jerked Pork Tenderloin with Mango Relish

PREP TIME
15 MINUTES

COOK TIME
25 MINUTES
(+ marinating time)

Jerked meat has a long and colorful history, and the term "jerk" refers to grilled meats (or vegetables) that have been flavored with a spicy-sweet mixture. In this dish, the coolness of the chilled relish is a sharp contrast with the heat of the spices in the cooked meat. So heap the mango relish high on your pork, and try to get a little relish in each succulent bite.

1. In a small bowl, combine the mango, cucumber, bell pepper, onion, and cilantro. Store the relish in the refrigerator in an airtight jar until you need it, up to 5 days.

2. Put the scallions, red wine vinegar, brown sugar, olive oil, lime juice, tamari sauce, garlic, allspice, cinnamon, black pepper, and cayenne pepper in a blender, and pulse until smooth. Transfer the mixture to a large resealable bag and add the pork. Seal the bag and marinate the pork in the refrigerator for at least 8 hours, turning occasionally.

3. Preheat the grill to medium-high.

4. Take the pork out of the bag and discard the leftover marinade. Grill the pork, turning, until it is cooked through, about 25 minutes. Remove to a cutting board and let stand for 10 minutes before slicing. Serve with the mango relish.

TIP: *Try this mango relish as a turkey burger topping, as a dip for shrimp, and stirred into Garden Gazpacho (page 129). If you can't find mangos, ripe peaches can be substituted. If you do not have a barbecue, preheat the oven to 400°F. Place an ovenproof skillet over medium-high heat, and pan sear the tenderloin so it is browned on all sides, about four minutes. Place the skillet in the oven and roast the tenderloin until it is cooked through, about 20 minutes.*

PAIR WITH . . . Sweet Potato Parsnip Mash (page 191)

1 mango, peeled, pitted, and diced

½ cup diced cucumber

½ red bell pepper, seeded, deribbed, and diced

¼ sweet onion, diced

1 tablespoon chopped fresh cilantro

2 scallions, white and green parts, chopped

1 tablespoon red wine vinegar

1½ teaspoons brown sugar

1 teaspoon olive oil

1 teaspoon freshly squeezed lime juice

1 teaspoon low-sodium tamari sauce

½ teaspoon minced garlic

¼ teaspoon ground allspice

Dash ground cinnamon

Dash freshly ground black pepper

Dash cayenne pepper

1 (10-ounce) pork tenderloin, trimmed of visible fat

PER SERVING
Calories: 325
Fat: 7.3g
Saturated fat: 2.0g
Protein: 35.8g
Carbohydrates: 27.5g
Sodium: 431mg
Fiber: 3.5g
Sugar: 20.6g

Spice-Rubbed Pork Tenderloin

GLUTEN-FREE
DAIRY-FREE
MAKE AHEAD
30 MINUTES

PREP TIME
10 MINUTES
(+ dry-rub time)

COOK TIME
15 MINUTES

Spices are an easy and economical method of infusing extra flavor into meats, poultry, and fish. Pork is a very mild-tasting meat, so a little oomph of heat and spice can transport this plain protein into a succulent treat. The spices in this rub can be further enhanced by lightly toasting the mixture in a skillet before rubbing them on the pork. Place the spices in a dry skillet over medium-high heat, and swirl them in the pan for just a few minutes, until they are fragrant and lightly toasted.

½ teaspoon ground cumin
½ teaspoon ground coriander
½ teaspoon ground cinnamon
¼ teaspoon allspice
¼ teaspoon ground ginger
1 (10-ounce) pork tenderloin
1 teaspoon olive oil

PER SERVING
Calories: 310
Fat: 14.0g
Saturated fat: 4.5g
Protein: 42.5g
Carbohydrates: 1.0g
Sodium: 92mg
Fiber: 0.0g
Sugar: 0.0g

1. In a small bowl, thoroughly combine the cumin, coriander, cinnamon, allspice, and ginger.

2. Rub the spice mixture generously all over the tenderloin. Refrigerate the tenderloin, covered, for at least 2 hours to let the flavors meld.

3. Heat the olive oil in a large skillet over medium-high heat. Cook the tenderloin until it is browned well on all sides and cooked through, about 15 minutes.

4. Let the pork rest on a cutting board for 10 minutes before slicing.

TIP: *Dried spices do not have an indefinite shelf life, so take the time each spring to look in your pantry for products that are past their best-before date. Your spices will not spoil, but they can certainly lose their potency after time, especially when stored in direct sunlight.*

PAIR WITH . . . Banana Basmati Rice (page 194)

Pork Tenderloin with Lemon Sauce

PREP TIME
15 MINUTES

COOK TIME
15 MINUTES

You might think you need some type of fancy mallet to pound out the pork tenderloin in this recipe. Although a mallet is a neat kitchen tool to have on hand, you can use a rolling pin just as easily. You still pound the pork out flat though; don't try to roll it! Make sure you place the meat between two sheets of plastic wrap or parchment before landing the first blow or you might end up with mashed pork all over the rolling pin.

1. In a small shallow bowl, combine the flour, thyme, salt, pepper, and half of the lemon zest. Dredge the pork pieces in the flour mixture.

2. Heat the olive oil in a large skillet over medium-high heat. Cook the pork, turning once, until browned and cooked through, about 8 minutes. Transfer the pork to a plate and cover loosely with aluminum foil to keep warm.

3. Add the chicken stock to deglaze the pan, stirring with a wooden spoon to scrape up the flavorful browned bits from the bottom. Reduce the heat to a low. Simmer the stock until it is reduced by half, about 3 minutes. Add the lemon juice, remaining zest, and parsley.

4. Serve the pork with the lemon sauce.

TIP: *Parsley is more than just a fresh green finish for your culinary masterpieces; it is also packed with healing properties. Parsley brims with vitamin K and is a decent source of vitamins A and C. This means parsley can cut the risk of cardiovascular disease and boost the immune system.*

PAIR WITH . . . Bulgur Herb Pilaf (page 194)

¼ cup all-purpose flour

1 teaspoon chopped fresh thyme, or ½ teaspoon dried thyme

Pinch sea salt

¼ teaspoon black pepper

Zest of ½ lemon, divided

1 (10-ounce) pork tenderloin, halved and pounded flat

1 teaspoon olive oil

½ cup low-sodium chicken stock

Juice of ½ lemon

1 tablespoon chopped fresh parsley

PER SERVING
Calories: 285
Fat: 7.5g
Saturated fat: 2.1g
Protein: 39.3g
Carbohydrates: 12.6g
Sodium: 217mg
Fiber: 0.6g
Sugar: 0.0g

Rack of Lamb with Apples

There is something elegant about lining up the gently curving bones of a perfectly roasted rack of lamb. A lamb rack does not seem like an everyday meal even though it is very easy to assemble and cook. This recipe is a classic preparation of lamb, crusting it with mustard and rosemary bread crumbs after a quick pan-sear. You can prep the lamb rack in the morning and store it in the refrigerator dressed in its breading for a quicker meal at the end of the day.

PREP TIME
15 MINUTES

COOK TIME
30 MINUTES

1 tablespoon whole-wheat bread crumbs

¾ teaspoon olive oil, divided

1 teaspoon chopped fresh rosemary, or ½ teaspoon dried rosemary, divided

Pinch sea salt

Pinch freshly ground black pepper

1 pound rack of lamb, frenched and trimmed

1 tablespoon Dijon mustard

1 apple, peeled, cored, and finely chopped

1 celery stalk, finely chopped

1 teaspoon cider vinegar

PER SERVING
Calories: 509
Fat: 41.9g
Saturated fat: 17.4g
Protein: 16.9g
Carbohydrates: 15.9g
Sodium: 303mg
Fiber: 2.9g
Sugar: 9.9g

1. Preheat the oven to 450°F.

2. In a small bowl, stir together the bread crumbs, ¼ teaspoon of olive oil, half of the rosemary, salt, and pepper.

3. Heat ½ teaspoon of olive oil a medium ovenproof skillet over medium-high heat. Cook the lamb meat-side down until browned, about 2 minutes. Turn the lamb over and spread the mustard over the meat. Press the bread crumb mixture onto the mustard. Place the skillet in the oven and roast the lamb to the desired doneness, about 20 minutes for medium rare.

4. Transfer the lamb to a plate and cover loosely with aluminum foil to keep warm.

5. Return the skillet to medium heat, taking care to use a hotpad on the hot handle. Add the apple, celery, and the remaining rosemary, and sauté for 2 minutes. Add the vinegar and simmer until the sauce looks syrupy, about 3 minutes.

6. Cut the lamb into chops and serve topped with the apples.

TIP: *"Frenched" is just a fancy way of saying that the bones of the lamb rack are exposed. You can get your butcher to do this or find lamb that is already trimmed in this manner. Frenching the rack creates a pretty visual impact when you cut the rack into chops after cooking it.*

PAIR WITH . . . Simple Roasted Baby Potatoes (page 191)

GLUTEN-FREE
DAIRY-FREE
30 MINUTES
ONE-POT

PREP TIME
2 MINUTES

COOK TIME
10 MINUTES

Harissa Lamb

Harissa is a commonly used North African condiment made from chiles, roasted red peppers, garlic, coriander, cumin, and caraway. It is a natural partner for lamb, one of the more popular proteins in North Africa, where you can take a live one home for roasting. Butchers even hang lamb heads in their shop window, so you know it is available and fresh. Harissa has heat and a smoky taste that compliments sandwiches, stews, and sauces. Find it online, in ethnic markets, or in most well-stocked supermarkets.

1. Spread the harissa on the lamb chops.

2. Heat the olive oil in a skillet over medium-high heat. Cook the lamb chops, turning at least once, for 4 minutes per side for medium.

3. Remove the lamb from the heat and let it rest for 5 minutes before thinly slicing the meat.

TIP: *Lamb is an excellent source of iron, zinc, and B vitamins such as thiamine and B$_{12}$. Modern farming techniques mean leaner animals with less fat, and the remaining fat is at least 50 percent monounsaturated, which is part of a healthy diet.*

PAIR WITH . . . North African–Spiced Carrots (page 188)

1 teaspoon harissa
2 (5-ounce) loin lamb chops, trimmed
1 teaspoon olive oil

PER SERVING
Calories: 292
Fat: 13.1g
Saturated fat: 4.0g
Protein: 40.0g
Carbohydrates: 1.0g
Sodium: 138mg
Fiber: 0.0g
Sugar: 0.7g

Juicy Lamb Burgers

DAIRY-FREE
MAKE AHEAD
30 MINUTES

PREP TIME
5 MINUTES

COOK TIME
12 MINUTES

This recipe has few ingredients because the flavor of grilled lamb needs no accoutrements to make it delicious. Lamb supports a very broad range of toppings, so don't be afraid to experiment in order to create a new family favorite. Some possible toppings include feta cheese, hummus, tahini, mayonnaise, hot chili sauce, fruit salad, and goat cheese.

½ pound lean ground lamb

1 egg white

½ onion, grated

3 tablespoons whole-wheat bread crumbs

¼ teaspoon freshly ground black pepper

2 whole-wheat buns

½ cup shredded lettuce

PER SERVING
Calories: 428
Fat: 10.4g
Saturated fat: 3.1g
Protein: 42.2g
Carbohydrates: 38.5g
Sodium: 429mg
Fiber: 6.0g
Sugar: 4.8g

1. In a large bowl, thoroughly mix together the lamb, egg white, onion, bread crumbs, and pepper. Form the mixture into 2 patties and store them, wrapped, in the refrigerator until you are ready to grill them.

2. Preheat a grill to medium-high.

3. Grill the lamb burgers until they are medium-well, about 6 minutes per side depending on thickness.

4. Toast the buns briefly on the grill. Put a lamb burger in each bun and top with lettuce.

TIP: *Serve these burgers without a bun and try rolled oats in the place of bread crumbs for a gluten-free option. Just make sure that the oats are labelled as gluten-free—some oat products contain wheat. If you do not have a barbecue, place a large skillet over medium high heat and pan sear the lamb burgers until they are the desired doneness, about six minutes per side for medium-well.*

PAIR WITH . . . Mixed Berries with Orange Cream (page 198)

WEEKEND RECIPES

Weekends are meant for leisurely mornings spent reading the paper while lingering over a perfectly browned frittata, or exploring interesting shops in a quaint town with a packed picnic lunch in the trunk of the car. Whatever your plans, from sporting events to working in the garden or doing a household to-do list together, weekends are for family.

Weekends are also the best time to explore facets of your culinary repertoire and try new recipes or cooking techniques. This doesn't mean you slave the day away over the stove, but it could involve searing sea scallops for the first time or creating the perfect gazpacho for weekend guests. Weekends are also fabulous for cooking together with healthy, quality ingredients because you haven't just rushed through the door after work. Collaboration in the kitchen should be enjoyable, and these weekend recipes are a perfect way to strengthen your connection over food and fun. No matter what your weekend plans, you will find a recipe to suit your needs. Whether you want a hearty sandwich made with summer vegetables, a stack of golden pancakes to dive into after sleeping in, or the perfect elegant dinner for special guests, you will discover the recipe here. You might have to take an extra day off on Monday to cook all the appealing choices that catch your eye.

Brunch

Artichoke Tomato Frittata

PREP TIME
5 MINUTES

COOK TIME
15 MINUTES

This recipe for the Italian version of an omelet bursts with juicy tomatoes and tender artichokes. Artichoke hearts are the edible flower bud of a thistle and are very high in fiber while low in calories and fat. They are also a good source of vitamins C and K, iron, and potassium. Artichokes are a heart-friendly ingredient, which explains their prevalence in the Mediterranean diet, one of the plans recommended for helping fight cardiovascular disease.

1. Preheat the oven to broil.

2. In a medium bowl, whisk together the eggs, cheese, basil, and pepper and set aside.

3. Heat the olive oil in a large ovenproof skillet over medium-high heat. Sauté the garlic and scallion for 1 minute. Add the artichoke hearts and cherry tomatoes and sauté for 3 minutes.

4. Remove the skillet from the heat and pour in the egg mixture. Return the skillet to the heat and cover. Heat the frittata without stirring until the egg mixture is set in the center, about 10 minutes.

5. Remove the skillet from the heat and place it under the broiler until the top is lightly browned, about 1 minute. Halve the frittata, and serve one half per person.

TIP: *If you have an allergy to ragweed or other related plants such as chrysanthemums, daisies, or arnica, artichokes may cause a severe allergic reaction. Substitute jarred hearts of palm or peeled broccoli stalks.*

PAIR WITH . . . Simple Roasted Baby Potatoes (page 191)

6 large eggs
¼ cup grated Parmesan cheese
1 tablespoon chopped fresh basil or 1½ teaspoons dried basil
Freshly ground black pepper
½ teaspoon olive oil
1 teaspoon minced garlic
1 scallion, white and green parts, cut into ¼-inch-thick slices
½ cup drained, quartered artichoke hearts
10 cherry tomatoes, halved

PER SERVING
Calories: 282
Fat: 19.1g
Saturated fat: 6.8g
Protein: 24.2g
Carbohydrates: 4.2g
Sodium: 427mg
Fiber: 0.8g
Sugar: 1.3g

Creamy Baked Eggs

GLUTEN-FREE
ONE-POT

PREP TIME
10 MINUTES
COOK TIME
30 MINUTES

Baking is one of the easiest and most elegant cooking methods for eggs; simply crack them into a ramekin, and place in an oven until the whites are set. The yolks will still be runny and rich. If you want to cut the cooking time down, you can use one egg per ramekin rather than two. You can also sprinkle these eggs with herbs, cheese, or even a spoon of salsa before baking them.

1 teaspoon butter

4 large eggs

Pinch sea salt

½ teaspoon freshly ground black pepper

1 tablespoon whipping cream

1 tablespoon chopped fresh parsley, or 1 teaspoon dried parsley

PER SERVING
Calories: 187
Fat: 14.6g
Saturated fat: 6.1g
Protein: 12.8g
Carbohydrates: 1.4g
Sodium: 247mg
Fiber: 0.0g
Sugar: 0.8g

1. Preheat the oven to 350°F. Grease two 8-ounce ramekins with butter.

2. Break 2 eggs into each ramekin. Season the eggs with the salt and pepper. Spoon half the cream over each ramekin.

3. Place the ramekins in a baking dish, and add hot water to reach halfway up the outside of the ramekins.

4. Bake until the eggs are set, about 30 minutes. Serve topped with the parsley.

TIP: *Baked eggs are also called shirred eggs or oeufs en cocotte. When you spoon the cream on the egg, it will coat the liquid whites and leave your unbroken yolks rising like islands out of the liquid. Don't miss this step—the cream prevents the whites from drying out in the oven.*

PAIR WITH . . . Wilted Greens (page 189)

PREP TIME
5 MINUTES

COOK TIME
25 MINUTES

Eggs Poached in Curry Sauce

This method of cooking eggs creates lovely little packages: runny yolks wrapped in snowy cooked whites surrounded by spicy curry sauce. It is a celebration of tastes and textures that are perfect for a special brunch dish. Make sure your curry sauce is not boiling when you spoon the eggs into it, or the whites will end up tough and stringy rather than fork-tender.

1. Heat the olive oil in a medium skillet over medium-high heat. Sauté the onion, garlic, and ginger until softened, about 5 minutes. Stir in the curry powder and pepper, and sauté for 1 minute. Stir in the tomatoes and cook for 5 minutes. Bring to a boil and add the coconut milk and cilantro. Cover and reduce the heat to low. Simmer for 10 minutes.

2. Make two deep indents in the sauce with a spoon. Crack an egg into each indent and cover the skillet. Cook until the whites are set, about 5 minutes.

3. Carefully spoon an egg and sauce onto 2 plates. Serve topped with the scallion.

TIP: *Use the freshest eggs possible when poaching. Eggs as little as a week old will have thinner whites, and since the whites need to contract around the yolks when the egg poaches, a fresh, thick white will create a more compact and uniform poached egg.*

PAIR WITH . . . Sautéed Lemon Pepper Mushrooms (page 190)

1 teaspoon olive oil
¾ cup chopped sweet onion
1 teaspoon minced garlic
1 teaspoon peeled, grated
    fresh ginger
1 teaspoon curry powder
Pinch freshly ground
    black pepper
1 (15-ounce) can sodium-free
    diced tomatoes
¼ cup light coconut milk
2 tablespoons chopped
    fresh cilantro
2 eggs
1 scallion, white and green
    parts, chopped

PER SERVING
Calories: 234
Fat: 14.7g
Saturated fat: 8.3g
Protein: 7.8g
Carbohydrates: 8.4g
Sodium: 112mg
Fiber: 2.3g
Sugar: 3.5g

Sweet Potato Pancakes

30 MINUTES

PREP TIME
10 MINUTES

COOK TIME
10 MINUTES

Pancakes are an easy fit for a leisurely weekend-morning meal, and this healthy version is naturally sweet, so you won't have to douse them in syrup. Sweet potatoes provide the lovely caramel taste and golden color of these fluffy pancakes, along with a healthy dose of important nutrients. Sweet potatoes are one of the highest sources of beta-carotene and contain over 200 percent of the recommended daily amount of vitamin A. In this recipe, the health benefits of beta-carotene are enhanced by the canola oil, which helps the body absorb this beneficial nutrient in higher quantities.

½ cup all-purpose flour
3 tablespoons
   whole-wheat flour
1 tablespoon brown sugar
1 teaspoon baking powder
Pinch sea salt
¼ teaspoon ground cinnamon
¼ teaspoon ground nutmeg
Pinch ground ginger
½ cup skim milk
½ cup cooked mashed
   sweet potato
1 egg
1 tablespoon canola oil
Nonstick cooking spray

PER SERVING
Calories: 322
Fat: 5.5g
Saturated fat: 1.1g
Protein: 10.9g
Carbohydrates: 56.8g
Sodium: 197mg
Fiber: 2.5g
Sugar: 11.2g

1. Sift the flour, whole-wheat flour, brown sugar, baking powder, salt, cinnamon, nutmeg, and ginger into a medium bowl, and whisk to mix well.

2. In a small bowl, whisk together the milk, sweet potato, egg, and oil until well combined and smooth. Add the sweet potato mixture to the dry ingredients and stir until just moistened.

3. Place a large skillet over medium heat and coat it lightly with cooking spray. Spoon ¼ cup batter per pancake into the skillet. Cook the pancakes until they have bubbles on the surface and edges are firm, about 3 minutes. Turn them over and cook about 2 minutes more.

4. Serve pancakes warm with fresh fruit.

TIP: *If you want to make a lovely lavender pancake for a special occasion or just for fun, try to find purple sweet potatoes at your local store. If you have never seen these unique vegetables before, it might be a surprise how purple they are when you peel the skin off. The exact shade will only be revealed when peeled, but they can be a vibrant, violet color.*

PAIR WITH . . . Chunky Applesauce (page 201)

Puffed Oven-Baked Apple Pancakes

Do you want to spend time enjoying a steaming cup of tea or coffee in the morning instead of flipping pancakes? These golden pancakes puff up all by themselves in the oven so you can relax. But don't be surprised if your inflated baked goods collapse a little when you get them onto a plate; this creates a layered effect and is quite normal. If you don't have two 5-inch pie plates, use a large pie plate to make one pancake, and then halve it after baking.

PREP TIME
10 MINUTES

COOK TIME
15 MINUTES

1. Preheat the oven to 400°F. Lightly coat two (5-inch) pie plates with cooking spray.

2. Whisk together the egg, flour, and buttermilk in a small bowl until very smooth. Pour the batter into the pie plates, dividing evenly. Bake until the pancakes are puffed and browned, about 15 minutes.

3. Serve immediately with Chunky Applesauce.

TIP: *The applesauce should be at room temperature at least, and slightly warm is best when spooned onto these pancakes.*

PAIR WITH . . . Nutmeg Baked Peaches (page 199)

Nonstick cooking spray
1 egg, lightly beaten
3 tablespoons
     all-purpose flour
3 tablespoons buttermilk
     or milk
1 recipe Chunky Applesauce
     (page 201)

PER SERVING
Calories: 109
Fat: 3.0g
Saturated fat: 0.9g
Protein: 5.2g
Carbohydrates: 15.7g
Sodium: 56mg
Fiber: 5.9g
Sugar: 4.8g

Simple Steel-Cut Oatmeal

MAKE AHEAD
ONE-POT

PREP TIME
5 MINUTES

COOK TIME
45 MINUTES TO
1 HOUR

Steel-cut oats are relatively unprocessed oat grains; they are chopped up, hulled, and toasted, and also called groats. Most people are more familiar with rolled oats, which are simply groats that have been steamed, then rolled flat. Steel-cut oats have about the same nutritional benefits as rolled oats, but the texture is completely different when cooked as a hot cereal. Rolled oats become very creamy, while steel-cut oats are chewy with a distinct nutty flavor. Steel-cut oats also take longer to cook, so they are not the first choice for people who are time challenged. However, if you love the taste and texture of steel-cut oats, cook them overnight in a slow-cooker for a hot meal first thing in the morning.

1 cup steel-cut oats

1½ cups water

½ cup skim milk

2 tablespoons brown sugar

2 tablespoons
dried cranberries

1 teaspoon flaxseed

PER SERVING
Calories: 220
Fat: 3.1g
Saturated fat: 0.0g
Protein: 7.8g
Carbohydrates: 40.2g
Sodium: 43mg
Fiber: 4.9g
Sugar: 12.4g

1. Put the oats, water, and milk in a medium saucepan, and stir to combine. Put the saucepan over medium-high heat. Cook, stirring occasionally, until the oats start to simmer.

2. Reduce the heat to low and cook, stirring occasionally, until the desired consistency is reached, about 45 minutes to 1 hour.

3. Serve the oatmeal warm, topped with brown sugar, cranberries, and flaxseed.

TIP: *You can top this cereal with an assortment of wholesome items, such as dried fruit, maple syrup, sunflower seeds, nuts, pumpkin seeds, and fresh fruit.*

PAIR WITH . . . Chunky Applesauce (page 201)

Fresh Fruit Pasta Salad

Sweet fruit and pasta might seem like an unusual mixture of ingredients, but this cold salad takes its origin from a famous dish, the Waldorf salad. It is not a perfect adaption, but the cut grapes, celery, crunchy pecans, and creamy dressing are very similar. Whole-wheat pasta adds bulk and texture to the dish, and the addition of oranges provides a lovely sweetness that balances out the other ingredients.

1. Remove enough zest from the orange to equal 1 teaspoon and set aside.

2. Using a sharp paring knife, peel the orange, making sure to trim off the bitter white pith. Working over a bowl to catch the juices, cut the segments out of the orange following each membrane; set aside. Measure 2 tablespoons of juice for the salad; set aside.

3. In a large bowl, combine the orange segments, pasta, celery, grapes, bell pepper, and scallion.

4. In a small bowl, mix the yogurt, orange juice and zest, and thyme. Add the dressing and the pecans to the salad and stir to combine. Refrigerate for at least 2 hours and serve.

TIP: *This recipe is spectacular with a lemon pasta. The added lemon zest in the pasta dough adds a zesty citrus component to the fruit in the salad.*

PAIR WITH . . . Coconut Energy Balls (page 184)

1 navel orange

4 cups cooked penne pasta

1 celery stalk, chopped

1 cup seedless green grapes, halved

½ red bell pepper, seeded, deribbed, and diced

1 scallion, white and green parts, chopped

¼ cup fat-free plain yogurt

2 tablespoons freshly squeezed orange juice

1 tablespoon chopped fresh thyme, or 1 teaspoon dried thyme

¼ cup chopped pecans

PER SERVING
Calories: 417
Fat: 5.3g
Saturated fat: 0.5g
Protein: 13.2g
Carbohydrates: 77.2g
Sodium: 64mg
Fiber: 7.6g
Sugar: 29.7g

Garden Gazpacho

GLUTEN-FREE
DAIRY-FREE
MAKE AHEAD
30 MINUTES
ONE-POT

PREP TIME
15 MINUTES
(+ chilling time)

The ingredients in this garden-fresh soup are not meant to be followed rigidly, because the best gazpacho is made with whatever is in season at the time you put it together. Use the freshest produce and herbs you can find. There are many versions of this refreshing soup with different ingredients such as bread, olives, tomato paste, and sherry vinegar, so feel free to play around. Most gazpacho recipes include a drizzle of good-quality olive oil when served in bowls. It's omitted here, but you can include it if you wish. However, try it without the oil first to see if the original version suits you better.

2 tomatoes, peeled and chopped

1 celery stalk, finely chopped

1 scallion, white and green parts, finely chopped

½ red bell pepper, seeded, deribbed, and finely chopped

½ cup chopped English cucumber

1 teaspoon minced garlic

¼ cup low-sodium tomato juice

⅓ cup low-sodium vegetable stock

1 tablespoon chopped fresh basil

Dash hot sauce (optional)

Freshly ground black pepper

1. Put the tomatoes, celery, scallion, bell pepper, cucumber, and garlic in a food processor (or blender) and pulse to create a chunky purée.

2. Transfer the tomato mixture to a medium bowl and stir in the tomato juice, stock, basil, and hot sauce (if using).

3. Season with pepper and refrigerate for at least 1 hour to let the flavors meld. Serve chilled.

TIP: *You can try peeling and deseeding the tomatoes to give the soup a smoother texture. Simply score the ends of the tomatoes with a knife and drop them into boiling water for 20 seconds. Peel off the skin and scoop out the seeds before chopping the tomato.*

PAIR WITH . . . Multigrain Chips (page 182)

PER SERVING

Calories: 50
Fat: 0.5g
Saturated fat: 0.0g
Protein: 2.3g
Carbohydrates: 10.8g
Sodium: 128mg
Fiber: 2.9g
Sugar: 6.3g

Blackened Salmon Po' Boy

PREP TIME
10 MINUTES

COOK TIME
15 MINUTES

The po' boy is a famous sandwich that originated in New Orleans when restaurateurs Clovis and Benjamin Martin created an inexpensive choice for unemployed striking streetcar drivers in 1929. The sandwich featured bits of cooked meat and gravy piled on crusty French bread. The sandwich has evolved into bread also stuffed with poultry and fresh, abundant seafood. This recipe uses juicy Cajun-spiced salmon, which also borrows from this rich culinary region.

1. Preheat the oven to 400°F.

2. Rub the seasoning all over the salmon fillets.

3. Heat the olive oil in a medium ovenproof skillet over medium-high heat. Cook the salmon on one side for 3 minutes without turning, then flip the fillets over carefully. Place the skillet in the oven and roast until the salmon is cooked through, about 8 minutes. Remove the salmon from the oven and set aside.

4. Split the bun lengthwise and toast for 3 minutes in the oven. Then spoon the yogurt into each bun, spreading it out. Top the yogurt with the salmon fillets. Top the salmon with spinach, tomato, and scallion.

TIP: *A true po' boy is only considered to be "dressed" when it is topped with shredded lettuce, tomatoes, pickles, and mayonnaise. You can try different combinations of greens and flavored mayo to create delectable options.*

PAIR WITH . . . Speedy Strawberry Ice Cream (page 198)

2 (4-ounce) skinless
salmon fillets
1 teaspoon Cajun seasoning
1 teaspoon olive oil
2 crusty whole-wheat rolls
2 tablespoons low-fat plain
Greek yogurt
1 cup shredded spinach
1 tomato, thinly sliced
1 scallion, white and green
parts, sliced

PER SERVING
Calories: 350
Fat: 14.0g
Saturated fat: 3.8g
Protein: 31.3g
Carbohydrates: 24.7g
Sodium: 641mg
Fiber: 4.4g
Sugar: 6.0g

Summer Lemon-Vegetable "Risotto"

GLUTEN-FREE
DAIRY-FREE
MAKE AHEAD
30 MINUTES
ONE-POT

PREP TIME
10 MINUTES

Don't panic when you see "risotto" in the title of this recipe. This is not the risotto that requires hours over the stove stirring in chicken stock. You will be mixing cold cooked rice with fresh-cut vegetables and a tart lemony dressing. The portions of this recipe are very generous, so if you are not overly famished, pack up half this dish for a simple, quick lunch the next day.

1 tablespoon freshly squeezed lemon juice

1 teaspoon grainy mustard

¼ teaspoon minced garlic

1 tablespoon olive oil

Sea salt

Freshly ground black pepper

2 cups cooked brown rice

1 cup chopped cooked chicken

1 scallion, white and green parts, cut into ⅛-inch-thick slices

12 cherry tomatoes, halved

½ cup green or wax beans, cut into 1-inch pieces

2 tablespoons chopped fresh basil, or 1 tablespoon dried basil

1. In a small bowl, whisk together the lemon juice, mustard, garlic, and olive oil. Season with salt and pepper.

2. In a large bowl, add the remaining ingredients and toss to combine.

3. Add the dressing to the rice mixture and stir to mix. Serve cold.

TIP: *You can use dried basil in this recipe, but the taste and fragrance of the fresh herb is better. Choose deep-green basil with no yellow or brown edges or spots on the leaves. To store a bunch of fresh basil, trim the stem ends; then stick the bunch in a glass of water on the counter as you would flowers. Cover the basil loosely with a plastic bag. It should keep for almost a week.*

PAIR WITH . . . Cheese Stuffed Pears (page 200)

PER SERVING
Calories: 509
Fat: 12.1g
Saturated fat: 1.9g
Protein: 31.4g
Carbohydrates: 73.5g
Sodium: 100mg
Fiber: 11.0g
Sugar: 19.6g

Baked Salmon Pockets

PREP TIME
20 MINUTES

COOK TIME
12 MINUTES

Layering vegetables, herbs, and a gorgeous piece of fresh fish in cute, simple-to-cook packages is fun and creates a delicious finished meal steamed in its own juices. You can create any combination of produce and fish with similar appealing results. The different vegetables should be cut into similar sizes so they cook evenly. The fish fillet cannot be very thick, or it will take too long to cook, leaving the vegetable bed soggy and overdone.

1. Preheat the oven to 350°F.

2. Cut two pieces of heavy aluminum foil 2 feet long and 1½ feet wide. Put them on the work surface and fold each piece in half lengthwise.

3. In a large bowl, toss together the potatoes, carrot, broccoli, leek, garlic, thyme, salt, pepper, and olive oil until well mixed. Put the vegetables in the center of the two pieces of foil, divided evenly. Place a salmon fillet on each pile of vegetables and squeeze half of the lemon juice over each piece. Fold the edges of the foil over and crimp to create loose packets.

4. Place the packets on a baking sheet. Bake until the salmon is done, about 12 minutes. Open carefully and serve.

TIP: *When you take the fish packets out of the oven, open them carefully with tongs because the escaping steam can burn your skin.*

PAIR WITH . . . Tropical Fruit Salad with Creamy Lime Sauce (page 198)

8 new potatoes, cooked and halved
1 carrot, peeled and sliced
1 stalk broccoli, cut into florets
1 leek, white and light-green parts, sliced and washed thoroughly
½ teaspoon minced garlic
1 tablespoon chopped fresh thyme, or 1 teaspoon dried thyme
Pinch sea salt
Large pinch freshly ground black pepper
1 tablespoon olive oil
2 (6-ounce) skinless salmon fillets
Juice of 1 lemon

PER SERVING
Calories: 492
Fat: 25.5g
Saturated fat: 4.8g
Protein: 37.3g
Carbohydrates: 29.5g
Sodium: 266mg
Fiber: 5.6g
Sugar: 5.2g

Citrus-Glazed Scallops

GLUTEN-FREE
30 MINUTES
ONE-POT

PREP TIME
10 MINUTES
COOK TIME
15 MINUTES

Scallops are an ideal choice for those who dislike seafood because they have a mild sweet taste and buttery texture. Scallops are best fresh, which means enjoying them between October and March, although you can buy them frozen as well. This recipe calls for sea scallops, which is the variety usually found in restaurants. You can also use bay scallops, a smaller, sweeter shellfish, if the larger scallop is not available. Double up on the bay scallops and cook them for one minute less, so they aren't overdone.

1 teaspoon olive oil

2 scallions, white and green parts, sliced thin

10 sea scallops, cleaned

1 teaspoon lemon zest

1 teaspoon orange zest

½ teaspoon lime zest

1 tablespoon chopped fresh thyme, or 1 teaspoon dried thyme

¼ cup freshly squeezed orange juice

2 tablespoons freshly squeezed lemon juice

1 tablespoon honey

2 tablespoons fat-free sour cream

PER SERVING
Calories: 225
Fat: 3.7g
Saturated fat: 0.6g
Protein: 26.4g
Carbohydrates: 20.2g
Sodium: 261mg
Fiber: 0.9g
Sugar: 13.0g

1. Heat the olive oil in a large skillet over medium-high heat. Sauté the scallions until softened, about 1 minute. Stir in the lemon, orange, lime zest, and thyme.

2. Add the scallops and cook for about 5 minutes, turning once. Add the orange and lemon juices and simmer for about 3 minutes.

3. Move the scallops to one side of the skillet and reduce the heat to low. Whisk the honey and sour cream into the citrus sauce and cook until the sauce thickens a little, about 4 minutes. Spoon the sauce to coat the scallops and serve immediately.

TIP: *Some scallops are treated with chemicals that make them suck up water so they can be sold as a heavier product. Look for scallops that are "dry," which means no chemicals were added. Dry natural scallops are a pretty pale-ivory color, whereas chemically treated shellfish are snowy white.*

PAIR WITH . . . Pistachio Rice Pilaf (page 194)

Lunch

PREP TIME
20 MINUTES
(+ refrigeration time)

Fennel Lentil Salad

A striking vegetable related to carrots and parsley and fennel looks like a bulbous bunch of celery with delicate fronds on the top. It is crunchy, fibrous, and has a distinct licorice taste and scent. This vegetable is a common ingredient in Italian cuisine and can be found in season from late fall to early spring, although it is available year-round. Fennel has the distinction of being a vegetable as well as an herb and spice. Note: Use fresh herbs here for the best flavor.

1. In a small bowl, whisk together the lemon juice, olive oil, garlic, and oregano. Season with salt and pepper.

2. In a large bowl, toss together the remaining ingredients until combined. Pour the dressing on the salad and toss to coat.

3. Refrigerate for 30 minutes before serving.

TIP: *A fennel bulb should never feel light for its size; that means it could be old and slightly dried out. Old fennel is woody in texture, which will wreck the freshness of this salad.*

PAIR WITH . . . Citrus Curd with Berries (page 199)

3 tablespoons freshly
  squeezed lemon juice
2 tablespoons olive oil
½ teaspoon minced garlic
1 tablespoon chopped
  fresh oregano
Sea salt
Freshly ground black pepper
¼ fennel bulb, shaved or cut
  into ⅛-inch-thick slices
1 tomato, diced
1 red bell pepper, seeded,
  deribbed, and julienned
1 scallion, white and green
  parts, ⅛-inch-thick slices
½ cup quartered water-packed
  artichoke hearts
2 tablespoons sliced
  black olives
2 cups canned green lentils,
  rinsed and drained
2 tablespoons chopped
  fresh parsley

PER SERVING
Calories: 287
Fat: 16.4g
Saturated fat: 2.9g
Protein: 10.0g
Carbohydrates: 27.4
Sodium: 305mg
Fiber: 11.1g
Sugar: 5.5g

Shrimp Black Bean Salad

PREP TIME
15 MINUTES
(+ refrigeration time)

The shrimp in this dish are chopped, so you get tender shellfish in every bite. Black beans are a nice addition because their deep color provides a striking contrast to the white shrimp, red tomatoes, and various shades of greens found in the other ingredients. Make sure you rinse the black beans very well under cool running water, as there can be a gel-like coating on canned beans that will make the salad mushy looking.

2 tablespoons
balsamic vinegar

1 tablespoon olive oil

1 teaspoon chili sauce

½ teaspoon ground cumin

¼ teaspoon ground coriander

1 cup cooked chopped shrimp

1 cup canned sodium-free
black beans, rinsed
and drained

1 cup diced English cucumber

8 cherry tomatoes, halved

½ red bell pepper, seeded,
deribbed, and diced

1 scallion, white and green
parts, chopped

1 tablespoon chopped
fresh cilantro

1. In a large bowl, stir together the vinegar, olive oil, chili sauce, cumin, and coriander. Add the remaining ingredients and toss to coat.

2. Chill the salad in the refrigerator for 1 hour. Serve cold.

TIP: *Use dried black beans if you have a little time and like the idea of controlling every aspect of your ingredients. Pick through the beans thoroughly for rocks by spreading the dried beans on a clean white cloth. Anything not black will show up easily. Afterward, rinse the beans; then prepare them according to the directions on the package.*

PAIR WITH . . . Citrus Curd with Berries (page 199)

PER SERVING
Calories: 380
Fat: 9.8g
Saturated fat: 1.1g
Protein: 32.1g
Carbohydrates: 47.2g
Sodium: 972mg
Fiber: 16.0g
Sugar: 16.8g

PREP TIME
20 MINUTES
(+ chilling time)

COOK TIME
35 MINUTES

Chicken Wild Rice Salad

Wild rice is a North American grass found growing naturally in several parts of the United States and Canada. This grain is considered sacred by many of the indigenous peoples of North America, and was not cultivated commercially until the 1950s. Most current varieties available are grown conventionally, not harvested in the wild. It has a nutty, rich flavor quite different than white or brown rice. Wild rice is a nutritional powerhouse and has almost double the protein and six times the folic acid of brown rice.

1. Add the wild rice, stock, and water to a medium saucepan over high heat and bring to a boil.

2. Reduce the heat to low, cover, and simmer until the rice, is tender, about 35 minutes. Rinse and drain the rice, and transfer it to a large bowl.

3. Add the chicken, lemon juice, bell pepper, scallions, green beans, carrot, cranberries, and almonds, and toss to combine.

4. In a small bowl, whisk together the olive oil, vinegar, mustard, and garlic until well combined. Season with pepper. Pour the dressing over the rice mixture, and mix well. Refrigerate for at least 1 hour before serving.

TIP: *Whenever possible, source wild rice that is organic and hand-harvested, if your budget supports that choice. Look for long-grain, unbroken rice grains, about an inch long. So-called short-grain wild rice has simply broken or been broken.*

PAIR WITH . . . Maple Pecan Tapioca Pudding (page 202)

1 cup wild and long-grain rice mixture, uncooked and rinsed

2 cups low-sodium chicken stock

1 cup water

2 (5-ounce) cooked skinless, boneless chicken breasts, cut into bite-size pieces

2 tablespoons freshly squeezed lemon juice

½ red bell pepper, seeded, deribbed, and diced

2 scallions, white and green parts, cut diagonally into ⅛-inch-thick slices

½ cup trimmed, halved green beans

½ cup shredded carrot

¼ cup dried cranberries

2 tablespoons slivered almonds

2 tablespoons olive oil

1 tablespoon rice vinegar

1 teaspoon Dijon mustard

½ teaspoon minced garlic

Freshly ground black pepper

PER SERVING
Calories: 622
Fat: 25.3g
Saturated fat: 4.5g
Protein: 41.7g
Carbohydrates: 53.9g
Sodium: 891mg
Fiber: 5.2g
Sugar: 5.4g

Grilled Vegetable Sandwich

This colorful meal is not a polite sandwich; it is a hearty creation that requires two hands to hold all the goodness on the bread. The sun-dried tomatoes provide a chewy texture and intense tomato burst. This sandwich would also be lovely with a drizzle of good-quality balsamic vinegar. If you do want to try this addition, try to find an aged vinegar—the taste will be richer and less astringent.

PREP TIME
15 MINUTES

COOK TIME
10 MINUTES

½ small eggplant, cut into ¼-inch slices

1 red bell pepper, seeded, deribbed, and cut into 1-inch-wide strips

1 zucchini, cut lengthwise into ¼-inch strips

½ red onion, cut into ¼-inch slices

1 teaspoon olive oil

Sea salt

Freshly ground black pepper

2 (1-inch-thick) slices French bread

4 sun-dried tomatoes

2 tablespoons crumbled low-fat goat cheese

1 tablespoon chopped fresh basil or 1 teaspoon dried basil

1. In a large bowl, toss the eggplant, bell pepper, zucchini, and onion with the olive oil, salt, and pepper.

2. Preheat a grill to medium-high heat.

3. Grill the vegetables until they are lightly charred and softened, about 6 minutes. Using tongs, transfer the vegetables to a plate.

4. Grill the bread lightly on both sides, about 1 minute total. Transfer the toasted bread to the work surface, and place 2 sun-dried tomatoes on each piece. Arrange the grilled vegetables on the bread, divided evenly. Sprinkle with the goat cheese and top with the basil.

5. Serve 1 open-faced sandwich each.

TIP: *If you do not have a grill, you can roast these vegetables in the oven at 400°F for about 25 minutes until tender and lightly browned. Turn them at least once during the roasting process to ensure all the sides get browned.*

PAIR WITH . . . Maple Pecan Tapioca Pudding (page 202)

PER SERVING
Calories: 288
Fat: 9.5g
Saturated fat: 4.6g
Protein: 14.0g
Carbohydrates: 39.5g
Sodium: 453mg
Fiber: 9.4g
Sugar: 12.7g

Salad in a Wrap

This is a vegetable lover's wrap because there is nothing to mask the fresh taste of the greens, tomato, and cucumber. There are no condiments in it: The avocado adds an appealing creaminess to the crunch of the veggies and acts as the glue to hold the whole wrap together. This adhesive effect is helped by refrigerating the wraps before serving.

1. Spread the tortillas on the work surface. Evenly layer the spinach, tomato, avocado, cucumber, and cheese on one-half of each tortilla, leaving a 1-inch border around the edge.

2. For each tortilla, fold the 1-inch edge over the filling and fold the side in to cover about half of the filling. Roll the tortilla tightly toward the empty half, creating a sealed bundle. Wrap each tortilla tightly in plastic wrap and refrigerate for at least 2 hours.

3. Unwrap the tortillas and cut each in half to serve, showing the filling.

TIP: *The spinach can be replaced by beet greens, kale, or shredded romaine, depending on your preference. This wrap would be tasty with all these greens, but the darker the green, the prettier the contrast when cut the wrap in half and reveal the filling.*

PAIR WITH . . . Chocolate Oat Bites (page 201)

2 (8-inch) whole-grain tortillas
1 cup shredded spinach
1 tomato, diced
½ avocado, pitted, peeled, and diced
¼ cup thinly sliced cucumber
¼ cup low-fat mozzarella

PER SERVING
Calories: 226
Fat: 14.3g
Saturated fat: 4.4g
Protein: 7.4g
Carbohydrates: 20.1g
Sodium: 261mg
Fiber: 6.2g
Sugar: 2.2g

Tuna Salad Pinwheels

These are tea sandwiches, garden-party treats with spiraling colors and a petite size that can be picked up and popped in your mouth in one tasty bite. One of the tricks to pinwheels that stay together is to make sure you squeeze out as much moisture as possible from the tuna so that it does not make the tortillas soggy. Also, you need to wrap the tortillas very tightly and chill them to set their shape. If you slice the pinwheels and they unwind a bit, place them, wrapped, back in the refrigerator for at least 30 minutes more.

PREP TIME
25 MINUTES
(+ chilling time)

1 (4-ounce) can water-packed tuna, drained

1 tablespoon fat-free plain Greek yogurt

1 teaspoon freshly squeezed lemon juice

Freshly ground black pepper

2 (8-inch) multigrain tortillas

½ cup shredded carrot

1 cup cucumber, shredded with the liquid squeezed out

½ red bell pepper, seeded, deribbed, and minced

2 tablespoons chopped fresh parsley

PER SERVING
Calories: 248
Fat: 4.8g
Saturated fat: 1.2g
Protein: 22.7g
Carbohydrates: 30.3g
Sodium: 519mg
Fiber: 6.8g
Sugar: 5.2g

1. In a small bowl, thoroughly combine the tuna, yogurt, lemon juice, and pepper.

2. Lay the tortillas on the work surface and spread the tuna mixture evenly over both, leaving a 1-inch border along the edge. Top the tuna evenly with the carrot, cucumber, and bell pepper. Sprinkle evenly with the parsley.

3. Roll up the tortillas tightly and wrap each in plastic wrap. Refrigerate for 30 minutes. Unwrap and trim off the empty tortilla ends. Cut each tortilla carefully into six pieces.

4. Arrange the pinwheels on two plates and serve 1 tortilla (six pieces) per person.

TIP: *There are many kinds of canned tuna in the grocery aisle, and it can be confusing to pick one for sandwiches, salads, and casseroles. White tuna is exclusively albacore tuna, which has a mild taste and firm texture. Light tuna is usually a variety of smaller tuna such as yellowfin and skipjack and is a stronger, fishier-tasting tuna. The best choice for these pretty pinwheels is solid white tuna.*

PAIR WITH . . . Velvety Chocolate Pudding (page 202)

PREP TIME
20 MINUTES

COOK TIME
8 MINUTES

Fish Tacos with Peach Salsa

Fish tacos have a colorful and varied history, but most versions hail from warm oceanfront areas and utilize freshly caught fish. Baja's Ensenada and San Felipe claim original ownership of this handheld meal of battered, deep-fried chunks of white fish stuffed in corn tortillas. This traditional version is still available in oceanside stands and restaurants up and down the West Coast, but the sandwich has also evolved into healthier versions. Fresh spiced fish, without the batter, is featured in this recipe, topped with simple shredded lettuce and a tangy peach salsa. You can almost hear the crashing waves and taste salt-kissed breezes when you bite into this yummy sandwich.

1. Combine the peach, bell pepper, scallion, lime juice, and cilantro in a small bowl. Set aside.

2. Rub the blackening spice all over the fish.

3. Heat the oil in a medium skillet over medium-high heat. Cook the fish about 4 minutes per side, until it is cooked through. Remove the fish from the skillet to a plate, and, using a fork, break up the fish.

4. Lay the tortillas on the work surface and divide the fish among them on one side. Top the fish with the lettuce and peach salsa. Fold the tortillas over and serve 2 per person.

TIP: *The best way to cook mahi mahi (or most fish) is over high heat for as little time as possible to produce a safe product. This dense, firm-textured fish does very well on the grill but can stick if it is not seasoned correctly with oil. Make sure you lightly coat the grill with oil by rubbing an oily cloth over the surface.*

PAIR WITH . . . Fresh Gingered Melon (page 198)

1 peach, pitted and diced

½ red bell pepper, seeded, deribbed, and finely diced

1 scallion, white and green parts, finely chopped

Juice of 1 lime

1 tablespoon chopped fresh cilantro

1 teaspoon blackening spice

1 (10-ounce) haddock or mahi mahi fillet

1 teaspoon olive oil

4 (6-inch) corn tortillas, at room temperature

1 cup finely shredded iceberg lettuce

PER SERVING

Calories: 297
Fat: 5.3g
Saturated fat: 1.0g
Protein: 30.9g
Carbohydrates: 31.8g
Sodium: 208mg
Fiber: 5.5g
Sugar: 7.7g

Stuffed Baked Potato

When you look at your plate, this overflowing potato will seem like the ultimate fattening indulgence. So you might be surprised to realize that this dish is very low in total fat and extremely low in saturated fat. Potatoes make very good containers for stuffing because they have a thick but tasty skin, and the flavor of this starchy vegetable is mild enough to combine well with everything. Try these chili-flavored delights the next time you are watching the big game on TV and want to dig into real filling food.

PREP TIME
10 MINUTES

COOK TIME
45 MINUTES

2 large baking potatoes

1 cup red kidney beans, rinsed and drained

1 tomato, chopped

1 scallion, white and green parts, sliced

1 teaspoon chili powder

1 teaspoon minced garlic

2 tablespoons shredded low-fat Cheddar cheese

2 tablespoons fat-free sour cream

PER SERVING
Calories: 563
Fat: 1.7g
Saturated fat: 0.0g
Protein: 28.1g
Carbohydrates: 114.6g
Sodium: 72mg
Fiber: 19.2g
Sugar: 6.1g

1. Preheat the oven to 350°F.

2. Pierce the potatoes with a fork, and bake them until tender, about 45 minutes.

3. While the potatoes are baking, place a small saucepan over medium-high heat and add the kidney beans, tomato, scallion, chili powder, and garlic. Bring to a boil; then reduce the heat to low, and simmer the bean mixture for 15 minutes to mellow the flavor. Remove from the heat.

4. Cut each baked potato lengthwise from end to end on one side, and press on the ends to open up the slit. Scoop out about half of the potato flesh, reserving it for another use. Spoon the chili mixture into the potatoes. Add the cheese and sour cream, divided evenly, between the potatoes.

TIP: *When looking for the perfect baking potato, select starchy varieties that have a mealy texture and thick skin. Russets typically are the best choice. Always make sure your potatoes are firm with no blemishes or wrinkles, and store them in a cool, dark place.*

PAIR WITH . . . Speedy Strawberry Ice Cream (page 198)

Frittata with Whole-Wheat Rotini

This recipe might be a culinary revelation for you and open up a new world of mixing pasta and eggs together in savory creations. The cooked pasta in this dish adds texture and a pleasant nutty taste, if you use a whole-wheat product. Whole-wheat pasta contains all the layers of the wheat kernel, so it is a fabulous source of fiber. The complex carbohydrates complement the high protein in the eggs to create a slow-release energy to get you through the day. Try other pasta shapes such as penne or farfalle if you don't have rotini in your cupboard.

1. Preheat the oven to 350°F.

2. In a medium bowl, whisk the egg whites, yogurt, chives, parsley, and pepper. Set aside.

3. Lightly coat a large ovenproof skillet with cooking spray and place it over medium-high heat. Sauté the garlic, scallion, and bell pepper until softened, about 3 minutes. Add the rotini and spread it evenly in the skillet. Pour the egg mixture over the pasta in the skillet. Shake the skillet to evenly distribute the eggs. Cook for 1 minute, without stirring, to set the bottom.

4. Place the skillet in the oven. Bake until the frittata is set and golden brown, about 20 minutes.

5. Remove the frittata from the oven. Serve hot or cold.

TIP: *You can store plain cooked pasta in your refrigerator in a tightly sealed container for up to 5 days. Pasta will also keep for six months in the freezer with no loss of texture as long as you cool it completely before sealing the container. Any trapped heat will make the pasta mushy.*

PAIR WITH . . . Chocolate Oat Bites (page 201)

8 large egg whites
½ cup low-fat plain yogurt
1 tablespoon chopped fresh chives
1 tablespoon chopped fresh parsley or 1 teaspoon dried parsley
Pinch freshly ground pepper
Nonstick cooking spray
1 teaspoon minced garlic
1 scallion, white and green parts, chopped
½ cup diced red bell pepper
2 cups cooked whole-wheat rotini

PER SERVING
Calories: 356
Fat: 3.1g
Saturated fat: 0.8g
Protein: 27.4g
Carbohydrates: 53.5g
Sodium: 307mg
Fiber: 5.8g
Sugar: 12.1g

Simple Dal

GLUTEN-FREE
DAIRY-FREE
MAKE AHEAD
ONE-POT

PREP TIME
5 MINUTES

COOK TIME
30 MINUTES

Dal (pronounced like "doll") sounds very exotic, but it is just a lentil porridge with chunky vegetables and spicy seasoning. This stew uses inexpensive ingredients to create a filling, thick pottage that can be a snack or appetizer or served with flatbread as a main dish. Dal is extremely popular with vegetarians because it is a very good source of protein and can contain many different ingredients, such as sweet potatoes, spinach, peppers, coconut, and dried fruit. You can find mild curry paste at most grocery stores in the international aisle.

½ cup red lentils

1 teaspoon olive oil

½ sweet onion, finely chopped

½ red bell pepper, seeded, deribbed, and finely chopped

1 tablespoon mild curry paste

2 cups low-sodium canned crushed tomatoes

1 teaspoon freshly squeezed lemon juice

¼ cup chopped fresh cilantro

PER SERVING
Calories: 240
Fat: 3.2g
Saturated fat: 0.0g
Protein: 14.5g
Carbohydrates: 39.9g
Sodium: 137mg
Fiber: 17.6g
Sugar: 3.0g

1. Add the lentils to a large saucepan, and cover with water by 1 inch. Bring to a boil over medium-high heat. Boil until the lentils are tender, about 15 minutes. Drain the lentils and transfer to a bowl.

2. Rinse out and dry the saucepan. Return the pan to the stove, and heat the olive oil over medium-high heat. Add the onion and bell pepper, and sauté until softened, about 3 minutes. Stir in the curry paste and cook for 1 minute. Add the tomatoes, lemon juice, and lentils. Cook, stirring occasionally, until heated through, about 10 minutes.

3. Serve topped with the cilantro.

TIP: *Unlike other legumes, lentils cook very quickly without presoaking. They do need to be rinsed thoroughly and picked through for grit and rocks. Do not mix old packages of lentils with newly purchased ones; older lentils tend to be drier and need more cooking time. You don't want your lentils to cook unevenly.*

PAIR WITH . . . Pistachio Rice Pilaf (page 194)

PREP TIME
10 MINUTES

COOK TIME
10 MINUTES

Vegetarian Pita Pizza

Pita pizzas are one of the quickest lunch ideas, and you can use all your favorite healthy topping ideas to create different pizzas every time. This recipe does not use a traditional spicy pizza sauce as a base, but it can certainly be substituted for the tomato in this recipe as long as it is a low-sodium product. Many commercial pizza sauces have a staggering amount of sugar and sodium, so take the time to read all the nutrition labels carefully before putting the sauce in your cart.

1. Preheat the oven to broil.

2. Place the pitas on the work surface, and spread each one with diced tomato. Top with the bell pepper, scallion, and basil. Sprinkle each pita with ½ cup mozzarella.

3. Put under the broiler and broil until the edges of the pizzas are lightly browned and the cheese is melted, about 6 to 8 minutes.

TIP: *If you are vegan, or have lactose intolerance, don't hesitate to substitute a vegan cheese made from soy, nut, or nutritional yeast ingredients.*

PAIR WITH . . . Ricotta Banana Split (page 200)

2 whole-wheat pitas

1 tomato, diced

½ red bell pepper, seeded, deribbed, and diced

1 scallion, white and green parts, chopped

1 tablespoon chopped fresh basil or 1 teaspoon dried basil

1 cup shredded fat-free mozzarella

PER SERVING
Calories: 256
Fat: 1.8g
Saturated fat: 0.0g
Protein: 19.2g
Carbohydrates: 41.8g
Sodium: 814g
Fiber: 6.0g
Sugar: 2.8g

Baked Tuna Burgers

Tuna is often thought to be used either in mayo-drenched sandwiches or seared very rare in a fine-dining restaurant. There is much more to this nutrient-packed ingredient, and these casual yet elegant burgers show a culinary middle ground appropriate for casual events or a special romantic evening for two. Make sure your tuna is as fresh as possible and packed on ice if you get it from a fishmonger. Ask to smell the fish before it is wrapped up, because if it is too "fishy," you might want to make a fresher selection.

PREP TIME
10 MINUTES

COOK TIME
15 MINUTES

Nonstick cooking spray

8 ounces skinless fresh, raw tuna, chopped

¼ onion, chopped

½ cup shredded carrot

½ red bell pepper, seeded, deribbed, and minced

½ teaspoon minced garlic

1 egg

3 tablespoons whole-wheat bread crumbs

Juice of ½ lemon

Pinch red pepper flakes

Pinch freshly ground black pepper

2 crusty buns

1 to 2 tablespoons Garlic and Herb Yogurt Dip (page 183)

1. Preheat the oven to 400°F. Line a baking sheet with parchment paper and lightly coat the parchment with cooking spray.

2. In a medium bowl, combine all the ingredients until well mixed. Form into two tuna patties and put them on the baking sheet.

3. Bake the tuna burgers, turning once, until browned and cooked through, about 15 minutes in total. Spread the buns with garlic and herb yogurt dip, and top with the burgers.

TIP: *Tuna is incredibly high in selenium, which is not a well-known mineral in the mainstream consumer market. Selenium is crucial for heart health and can help prevent several types of cancer, such as stomach, skin, and lung. Since selenium can slow blood clotting, it is a good idea not to ingest too much of this mineral if you are on medications designed to do the same thing, such as aspirin and heparin.*

PAIR WITH . . . Green Beans with Pecans (page 190)

PER SERVING
Calories: 383
Fat: 5.9g
Saturated fat: 0.8g
Protein: 37.3g
Carbohydrates: 43.0g
Sodium: 478mg
Fiber: 3.1g
Sugar: 6.8g

Supper

PREP TIME
5 MINUTES

COOK TIME
25 MINUTES

Mushroom and Scallion Frittata

Who says you can't have eggs for dinner, especially this mushroom-studded frittata? There are very few ingredients in this dish, so the quality and type of mushroom used is crucial to the finished taste and texture. Plain mild button mushrooms produce a pleasing, almost buttery dish that is as comforting as a warm sweater on a chilly day. Using earthy shiitakes or fruity oyster mushrooms can create a sophisticated flavor that would not be out of place in a French bistro. Choose your favorites or mix the mushrooms up for a truly unique frittata.

1. Preheat the oven to 350°F.

2. Heat the olive oil in a medium ovenproof skillet over medium heat. Sauté the scallions and mushrooms until they are very soft, about 15 minutes.

3. In a medium bowl, whisk together the eggs and pepper. Pour the eggs over the vegetables, stirring for about 3 minutes to disperse the vegetables. Cook for 4 minutes more, without stirring, to set the eggs a little.

4. Bake in the oven until completely set and golden brown, about 10 minutes. Serve warm or cold.

TIP: *Do not use portobello mushrooms in your frittata unless you scoop out the dark gills with a spoon before sautéing them, or the frittata will have an unpleasant grey hue. Portobellos taste wonderful but impart a dark murky look to other ingredients if the gills are left intact.*

PAIR WITH . . . Broiled Tomatoes (page 192)

1 tablespoon olive oil

4 scallions, white and green parts, cut into ¼-inch-thick slices

2 cups thinly sliced button or wild mushrooms

4 eggs

Pinch freshly ground black pepper

¼ cup grated Parmesan cheese

PER SERVING
Calories: 391
Fat: 28.0g
Saturated fat: 11.7g
Protein: 31.8g
Carbohydrates: 7.2g
Sodium: 652mg
Fiber: 1.5g
Sugar: 2.6g

Eggplant Paprikash

GLUTEN-FREE
MAKE AHEAD
ONE-POT

PREP TIME
20 MINUTES

COOK TIME
30 MINUTES

This fragrant mixture is a simple, filling stew that uses eggplant instead of meat for the base. Eggplant is a very meaty-textured vegetable, so it can take strong spices easily and satisfy the hungriest diner. Many people dislike this shiny, purple vegetable because it has a strange spongy texture and can be bitter if it is not prepared correctly. Sprinkling sliced or cubed eggplant with salt and letting it sit for at least 30 minutes removes the bitterness in most cases. If you do not like adding extra salt to your meals, make sure you buy young, freshly harvested eggplants, as they are not as bitter.

Nonstick cooking spray
½ onion, peeled and sliced
1 teaspoon minced garlic
1 tablespoon smoked paprika
Pinch salt
1 (1-pound) eggplant, cut into 1-inch cubes
1 red bell pepper, seeded, deribbed, and cut into ¼-inch-thick slices
½ cup low-sodium vegetable stock
1 tomato, coarsely chopped
2 tablespoons fat-free sour cream

1. Lightly coat a large skillet with cooking spray and place over medium heat. Sauté the onion until it is lightly browned, about 5 minutes. Add the garlic, paprika, and salt, and sauté for about 2 minutes. Add the eggplant, bell pepper, stock, and tomato. Bring to a boil; then reduce the heat to low. Cover and simmer, stirring occasionally, until the eggplant is very tender, about 20 minutes.

2. Stir in the sour cream and simmer for 1 more minute.

TIP: *Low-sodium tomato juice can be used in place of the vegetable stock if you want a thicker, more flavorful stew. Most prepared vegetable stocks have very little taste unless you spend a little more money on the organic version.*

PAIR WITH . . . Cinnamon Couscous (page 193)

PER SERVING
Calories: 134
Fat: 1.7g
Saturated fat: 0.0g
Protein: 5.0g
Carbohydrates: 28.2g
Sodium: 127mg
Fiber: 13.0g
Sugar: 12.5g

PREP TIME
15 MINUTES

COOK TIME
10 MINUTES

Sesame Vegetable Stir-Fry

The subtle crunch and distinct nutty flavor supplied by these tiny seeds is a hallmark of Asian cuisine. Sesame oil is a centuries-old ingredient prized because it resists rancidity and is a good source of healthy, monounsaturated fats. When using sesame oil, keep in mind that the taste is very strong, so a little goes a very long way. You can choose either light or dark (toasted) sesame oil for your stir-fries.

1. Stir together the water, tamari sauce, honey, and ginger in a small bowl.

2. Heat the sesame oil in a large skillet over medium-high heat. Stir-fry the broccoli, carrot, celery, and bell pepper until the vegetables are crisp-tender, about 4 minutes. Add the mushrooms and zucchini, and stir-fry for 4 minutes. Add the sauce and toss to coat. Stir-fry until the sauce thickens, about 2 minutes.

3. Serve topped with the sesame seeds.

TIP: *Sesame seeds come in different colors, but all taste lovely with this stir-fry. The golden ones are probably what you will use most, but black and red sesame seeds are readily available as well for an interesting look as a garnish.*

PAIR WITH . . . Fruit Tarts   (page 199)

2 tablespoons water

1 tablespoon low-sodium tamari sauce

1 tablespoon honey

1 teaspoon peeled, grated fresh ginger

1 teaspoon sesame oil

1 stalk broccoli, cut into small florets

1 carrot, cut crosswise into ¼-inch-thick slices

1 celery stalk, cut crosswise into ¼-inch-thick slices

1 red bell pepper, seeded, deribbed, and julienned

½ cup sliced button mushrooms

1 small zucchini, cut crosswise into ¼-inch-thick slices

2 teaspoons sesame seeds

PER SERVING
Calories: 136
Fat: 4.3g
Saturated fat: 0.6g
Protein: 4.9g
Carbohydrates: 21.4g
Sodium: 402mg
Fiber: 4.2g
Sugar: 14.4g

Pasta Primavera

MAKE AHEAD
30 MINUTES
ONE-POT

PREP TIME
10 MINUTES
COOK TIME
15 MINUTES

Primavera is an Italian word that means "spring." In a culinary sense it usually indicates that a pasta primavera is filled with fresh vegetables of all types. This recipe delivers on that promise with green beans, red bell peppers, and sweet onions in an herbed white-wine sauce. This recipe is not a delicate appetizer pasta, though; hearty multigrain pasta and filling white kidney beans create a satisfying main meal.

1 teaspoon olive oil

1 teaspoon minced garlic

½ sweet onion, chopped

1 red bell pepper, seeded, deribbed, and julienned

½ cup green beans, trimmed and cut into 1-inch pieces

1 cup white kidney beans, rinsed and drained

2 tablespoons dry white wine

Juice and zest of ½ lemon

1 tablespoon chopped fresh thyme, or 1 teaspoon dried thyme

Pinch sea salt

Pinch freshly ground black pepper

Pinch red pepper flakes

1 teaspoon butter

3 cups cooked multigrain spaghetti

2 tablespoons grated Parmesan cheese

1. Heat the olive oil in a large skillet over medium heat. Sauté the garlic, onion, and bell pepper until softened, about 3 minutes. Add the green beans and sauté for 1 minute. Add the kidney beans, white wine, lemon juice and zest, thyme, salt, pepper, and red pepper flakes. Bring to a boil; then reduce the heat to low. Simmer the vegetables until crisp-tender, about 5 minutes.

2. Add the butter and pasta to the vegetable mixture, stirring gently to combine until the pasta is heated through, about 2 minutes. Serve topped with the Parmesan.

TIP: *If you want to make an exact amount of pasta for this recipe, cook 6 ounces of dry spaghetti to yield 3 cooked cups. Bring 6 cups of cold water to a boil and cook your pasta, stirring frequently until the pasta is* al dente *(meaning firm when bitten, or "to the tooth" in Italian). You can add salt to the water after it has boiled to provide seasoning, but never add oil, because it creates a pasta that does not allow the sauce to stick.*

PAIR WITH . . . Speedy Strawberry Ice Cream (page 198)

PER SERVING

Calories: 558
Fat: 12.6g
Saturated fat: 5.8g
Protein: 28.6g
Carbohydrates: 85.1g
Sodium: 662mg
Fiber: 18.2g
Sugar: 9.4g

PREP TIME
15 MINUTES

COOK TIME
10 MINUTES

Quick "Chow Mein"

If you look at menus in authentic Chinese restaurants, you will realize that the chow mein prepared in this recipe is not a traditional variation. Chow mein ordinarily includes an abundance of fried noodles that are tossed with vegetables and spicy sauce. Here, bean sprouts provide a noodlelike appearance without any of the fat, calories, or gluten. You might find yourself taking any leftovers to work the next day because chow mein, noodles or not, is just as tasty cold.

1. Whisk the stock, tamari sauce, cornstarch, sugar, ginger, and red pepper flakes together in a small bowl until well blended. Set aside.

2. Heat the sesame oil in a large skillet over medium-high heat. Stir-fry the celery, carrot, mushrooms, and bell pepper until the vegetables are crisp-tender, about 4 minutes. Add the snow peas and bean sprouts and stir-fry for an additional 3 minutes.

3. Move the vegetables to the side of the skillet and pour in the sauce. Whisk until the sauce is thick and glossy, about 2 minutes. Toss the sauce with the vegetables to combine.

4. Serve topped with the scallions and sesame seeds.

TIP: *Bean sprouts should be cooked well in a hot pan to ensure that they do not have any bacterial contamination. If you have any sprouts left over after making this dish, do not use them raw on salads unless you sprouted them yourself.*

PAIR WITH . . . Pecan Honey Bananas (page 200)

¾ cup vegetable stock

3 tablespoons low-sodium tamari sauce

2 tablespoons cornstarch

1 tablespoon sugar

1 teaspoon peeled, grated fresh ginger

Pinch red pepper flakes

1 teaspoon sesame oil

2 stalks celery, sliced

1 carrot, cut crosswise into ⅛-inch-thick slices

1 cup sliced button mushrooms

1 red bell pepper, seeded, deribbed, and julienned

½ cup snow peas, trimmed

1 cup bean sprouts, washed thoroughly

2 scallions, white and green parts, cut into ⅛-inch-thick slices

1 teaspoon sesame seeds

PER SERVING
Calories: 207
Fat: 4.1g
Saturated fat: 0.6g
Protein: 11.1g
Carbohydrates: 32.1g
Sodium: 954mg
Fiber: 4.8g
Sugar: 14.7g

Tuna Steaks Provençal

PREP TIME
15 MINUTES
COOK TIME
20 MINUTES

Tuna steaks are usually served rare after searing them very quickly in a very hot skillet or on a grill. Searing traps the moisture of the flesh inside, creating a juicy steak. The reason most professional chefs cook this fish rare, or close to it, is because tuna is extremely lean, and dries out very quickly when cooked. The muscle fibers in the fish contract as it cooks, so well-done tuna will be chewy and unpleasant. If rare scares you too much, at least try your steaks medium-rare to see the difference.

1 teaspoon olive oil, divided

1 red bell pepper, seeded, deribbed, and diced

½ red onion, cut into ¼-inch-thick slices

½ teaspoon minced garlic

1 tomato, diced

¼ cup white wine

4 Kalamata olives, pitted and chopped

1 tablespoon chopped fresh rosemary, or 1 teaspoon dried rosemary

2 (4-ounce) tuna steaks

PER SERVING
Calories: 298
Fat: 10.7g
Saturated fat: 2.4g
Protein: 35.1g
Carbohydrates: 8.4g
Sodium: 139mg
Fiber: 2.6g
Sugar: 4.3g

1. Preheat the oven to 400°F.

2. Heat ½ teaspoon of olive oil in a medium skillet over medium-high heat. Sauté the bell pepper, onion, and garlic until softened, about 3 minutes. Stir in the tomato and white wine, and bring to a boil. Reduce the heat to low and simmer until the sauce thickens slightly, about 4 minutes. Add the olives and rosemary. Remove the sauce from the heat and set aside.

3. Heat the remaining ½ teaspoon of olive oil in an ovenproof skillet over high heat. Sear the tuna steaks for 1 minute on each side.

4. Place the pan in the oven and roast the fish until it is opaque, about 8 minutes.

5. Remove from the oven and serve the fish topped with the sauce.

TIP: *Always rinse fish under cold running water, even if it is just purchased, before using it in a recipe. This will remove residue of any type from the surface of the tuna, including bacteria from anyone handling it* en route *to your kitchen.*

PAIR WITH . . . Wilted Greens (page 189)

Tuna Noodle Casserole

This unpretentious dish is a staple in many homes because it is quick and uses ingredients you probably already have on hand. Unfortunately, tuna casserole has some unhealthy connotations because there are so many fat- and sodium-laden recipes, including several calling for a crushed-potato-chip topping. Tuna casserole can be lighter, and since it freezes well, you can make a double batch for the freezer when you want a break from cooking after work.

1. Preheat the oven to 350°F.

2. Melt the butter in a large saucepan over medium-high heat. Add the mushrooms and shallots, and sauté until the shallots are translucent, about 3 minutes. Whisk the flour into the mushroom mixture until it looks pasty, about 1 minute. Pour in the milk and whisk until the sauce thickens, about 3 minutes. Whisk in the Parmesan, parsley, and salt, and remove the sauce from the heat.

3. Stir the macaroni and tuna into the sauce and season with pepper. Spoon the mixture into a 6-by-6-by-3-inch baking dish, and bake until edges are bubbly, about 20 minutes.

TIP: *There are several classic sauces in a professional cook's repertoire that take skill and practice to prepare. It is interesting that one of these sauces, the béchamel, is the base of the casual tuna casserole. This recipe does not produce a truly authentic béchamel, but the milk-based cheese sauce thickened with a flour-and-butter roux is close enough to say you know a few French cooking techniques.*

PAIR WITH . . . Fruit Tarts (page 199)

1 teaspoon butter

⅔ cup sliced button mushrooms

2 shallots, chopped

1 tablespoon all-purpose flour

⅔ cup skim milk

1 tablespoon grated Parmesan cheese

1 tablespoon chopped fresh parsley, or 1 teaspoon dried parsley

Pinch sea salt

3 cups cooked whole-wheat macaroni

1 (6-ounce) can water-packed solid white tuna, drained and broken into chunks

Freshly ground black pepper

PER SERVING
Calories: 478
Fat: 6.9g
Saturated fat: 3.6g
Protein: 41.5g
Carbohydrates: 65.7g
Sodium: 356mg
Fiber: 6.2g
Sugar: 6.1g

Shrimp and Spinach Linguine

DAIRY-FREE
30 MINUTES
ONE-POT

PREP TIME
10 MINUTES

COOK TIME
15 MINUTES

The simple prettiness of this pasta will please even the harshest critic, and the ease of preparation will please the most inexperienced cook. You can place this restaurant-quality dish on your table in less than 30 minutes; if you have your ingredients prepared in advance, that time is even shorter. Even if you are not enamored with spicy food, do not omit the pinch of red pepper flakes from the recipe. That hint of heat elevates this dish to sublime without overpowering the taste buds.

1 teaspoon olive oil, divided

1 teaspoon minced garlic

1 red bell pepper, seeded, deribbed, and thinly sliced

16 (31/35 count) medium shrimp, peeled, deveined, and halved lengthwise

2 tomatoes, coarsely chopped

Juice and zest of 1 lemon

Pinch red pepper flakes

2 cups packed spinach

3 cups cooked whole-grain linguine

1 scallion, white and green parts, cut into ⅛-inch-thick slices

PER SERVING
Calories: 445
Fat: 5.7g
Saturated fat: 0.6g
Protein: 50.1g
Carbohydrates: 51.7g
Sodium: 1521mg
Fiber: 9.9g
Sugar: 11.2g

1. Heat ½ teaspoon of olive oil in a large skillet over medium-high heat. Sauté the garlic and bell pepper until softened, about 3 minutes. Using a slotted spoon, transfer the vegetables to a plate.

2. Add the remaining ½ teaspoon of olive oil to the skillet, and sauté the shrimp until opaque, about 5 minutes.

3. Add the sautéed vegetables, tomatoes, lemon juice and zest, and red pepper flakes. Reduce the heat to low, and add the pasta and scallions. Toss to combine and simmer until the pasta is heated through, about 4 minutes.

TIP: *Red pepper flakes add a kick to any dish, but they also add some significant health benefits as well. These hot flakes can boost metabolism and help suppress appetite, which can be very beneficial if you are trying to lose weight or maintain your current physique. Red pepper flakes can also help prevent blood clots and clear up any congestion issues. If you have ever experienced a runny nose after consuming a spicy meal, this clearing of the sinuses will come as no surprise.*

PAIR WITH . . . Cheese-Stuffed Pears (page 200)

PREP TIME
15 MINUTES

COOK TIME
50 MINUTES

Chicken Meat Loaf

This pretty orange- and green-flecked loaf has a subtle heat from the fresh ginger. Lean ground chicken cooked up with the grated carrot and finely chopped mushrooms creates a pleasing fork-tender texture. You can substitute several different grated vegetables in this loaf with stellar results, such as parsnip, sweet potato, zucchini, and celery root. Take the time to experiment on a leisurely day off to see which combination suits your palate best.

1. Preheat the oven to 350°F. Line an 8-by-5-inch loaf pan with parchment paper.

2. Place all the ingredients in a large bowl and mix well using your hands. Press the meat mixture into the pan, making a loaf with room around the sides where the juices can collect.

3. Bake the meatloaf until it is cooked through and golden brown, about 50 minutes. Remove from the oven and let stand for about 10 minutes. Pour off any oil. Place the meatloaf on a platter and cut into serving slices.

TIP: *Mushrooms are the only source of vitamin D found in fruits and vegetables, so they can be a great addition to any healthy diet, especially for people living in Northern regions that don't get a great deal of year-round sun. Mushrooms are also a rich source of B vitamins, antioxidants, and iron.*

PAIR WITH . . . North African–Spiced Carrots (page 188)

1 pound lean ground chicken

1 egg white

1 scallion, white and green parts, chopped

1 teaspoon minced garlic

1 teaspoon peeled, grated fresh ginger

1 cup finely chopped button mushrooms

1 cup grated carrot

Pinch freshly ground black pepper

1 tablespoon chopped fresh thyme, or 1 teaspoon dried thyme

PER SERVING
Calories: 347
Fat: 12.4g
Saturated fat: 4.0g
Protein: 49.8g
Carbohydrates: 8.5g
Sodium: 319mg
Fiber: 2.4g
Sugar: 3.6g

Chicken Broccoli Casserole

PREP TIME
15 MINUTES

COOK TIME
30 MINUTES

In the 1980s everyone was making a casserole called chicken divine that was decadently cheesy but horrifically bad for your health. This recipe is a healthier version of that popular dish, with all the flavor and much less fat. The original chicken divine did not include the brown rice found in this one-pot meal. It is very important not to overcook the broccoli in this casserole, because it provides vibrant green accents and a nice subtle crunch.

1 stalk broccoli, cut into small florets

1 cup diced cooked chicken breasts

3 cups cooked brown rice

1 teaspoon butter

1 teaspoon all-purpose flour

1 cup low-fat chicken stock

¼ cup grated Parmesan cheese

½ teaspoon ground nutmeg

2 tablespoons whole-wheat bread crumbs

PER SERVING
Calories: 594
Fat: 15.8g
Saturated fat: 5.9g
Protein: 38.6g
Carbohydrates: 74.0g
Sodium: 453mg
Fiber: 3.6g
Sugar: 1.3g

1. Preheat the oven to 350°F.

2. Bring about 3 cups of water to a boil in a small saucepan and blanch the broccoli for 1 minute. Drain the broccoli and transfer to a large bowl. Add the chicken and rice to the bowl, and toss to mix.

3. Put the saucepan back over medium-high heat and melt the butter. Add the flour and stir to combine. Slowly pour in the chicken stock and whisk until the sauce thickens, about 5 minutes. Stir in the Parmesan and nutmeg.

4. Pour the sauce over the rice mixture and stir to mix well. Spoon the mixture into an 8-by-8-inch baking dish, and sprinkle the bread crumbs evenly over the top of the casserole. Bake until bubbly and lightly browned, about 20 minutes.

TIP: *Broccoli is a cruciferous vegetable and considered to be a nutritional superstar. It is high in fiber, vitamin C, potassium, calcium, and folic acid. The range of nutrients in broccoli means it has a positive effect upon every system in the body. In particular, broccoli can reduce high blood pressure and the damaging symptoms of arthritis and Alzheimer's while cutting the risk of several cancers.*

PAIR WITH . . . Chunky Applesauce (page 201)

Chicken Parmesan

Golden, crispy-breaded chicken breasts covered with ripe tomatoes and sweet basil with a sprinkling of gooey melted cheese—who wouldn't want to linger lovingly over that meal? This baked recipe has much less fat than the chicken Parmesan found in most old cookbooks and on restaurant menus. Original recipes usually call for deep-fried, breaded chicken topped with thick tomato sauce and heaps of cheese, which is great if you have no plans for a long, healthy life. You will be surprised how decadent this recipe tastes.

1. Preheat the oven to 400°F. Lightly coat a baking sheet with cooking spray.

2. In a small shallow bowl, whisk the egg with 1 tablespoon water. In another small shallow bowl, stir together the bread crumbs and 2 tablespoons of the Parmesan.

3. Pat the chicken pieces dry and dredge them in the egg mixture, shaking off the excess.

4. Dredge the chicken in the bread crumb mixture. Place the breaded chicken pieces on the prepared baking sheet and lightly spray with cooking spray.

5. Bake the chicken pieces for 15 minutes on one side. Turn the chicken over, and top each piece evenly with the tomato and basil. Evenly sprinkle the chicken with the remaining 6 tablespoons of Parmesan. Continue to bake until the chicken is cooked through and the cheese is melted, about 10 minutes.

TIP: *Parmesan cheese is often found in healthier recipes along with Asiago and Romano. The strong pungent taste of these hard Italian cheeses is a fabulous flavor base. Parmesan cheese has many of the nutritional benefits of milk, even in small quantities; it takes about 84 cups of milk to make 2 pounds of Parmesan.*

PAIR WITH . . . Sautéed Lemon Pepper Mushrooms (page 190)

Nonstick cooking spray

1 egg

2 tablespoons whole-wheat bread crumbs

½ cup grated Parmesan cheese, divided

2 (6-ounce) boneless chicken breasts, halved crosswise to get 4 thin cutlets

1 tomato, diced

1 tablespoon chopped fresh basil, or 1 teaspoon dried basil

PER SERVING
Calories: 358
Fat: 9.1g
Saturated fat: 0.9g
Protein: 59.5g
Carbohydrates: 8.6g
Sodium: 285mg
Fiber: 1.4g
Sugar: 3.0g

Pork Stew with Dark Beer

PREP TIME
15 MINUTES

COOK TIME
**1 HOUR AND
45 MINUTES**

Pork stew has a long and varied history spanning the entire British Isles, Germany, and South America. Obviously these very different countries use an assortment of diverse ingredients to complement the pork, including vegetables, fruit, grains, and spices. The addition of beer in this recipe creates a very rich sauce, especially if you use a dark creamy beer like Guinness. You will not be using the entire can or bottle for the stew, so either drink it yourself or have a beer-loving friend present to take it off your hands. You can also use leftover beer in a light beer batter if the beer is not dark. Pilsner-style lagers or pale ales are not recommended for this recipe, as they will impart an acidity or bitterness from the hops they contain.

½ pound boneless pork shoulder, cut into 1-inch pieces
1 tablespoon olive oil
1 onion, diced
2 carrots, peeled and diced
1 tart apple, peeled, cored, and diced
2 teaspoons minced garlic
1 tomato, diced
1 cup low-sodium chicken stock
½ cup dark beer
½ teaspoon ground cinnamon
Freshly ground black pepper

PER SERVING
Calories: 353
Fat: 11.2g
Saturated fat: 2.4g
Protein: 32.3g
Carbohydrates: 26.9g
Sodium: 147mg
Fiber: 5.4g
Sugar: 14.7g

1. Heat the olive oil in a large saucepan over medium-high heat. Brown the pork, stirring, for about 5 minutes and then remove with a slotted spoon to a plate.

2. Add the onion, carrots, and apple to the saucepan, and sauté until they are softened, about 8 minutes. Add the garlic and sauté for an additional 2 minutes. Stir in the tomato, stock, beer, cinnamon, and the browned pork with accumulated juices, and season with pepper. Bring the stew to a boil; then reduce the heat to low. Simmer, partially covered, stirring occasionally, until the pork is very tender, about 1½ hours.

TIP: *If your stew tastes a little acidic, try cutting the taste with a teaspoon of brown sugar or another sweetener. Think about how a bit of sugar mellows out an acidic tomato sauce; the same is true for this stew if the taste is not right.*

PAIR WITH . . . Chunky Applesauce (page 201)

Pecan-Crusted Pork Chops

Pecans are considered to be a nutritious tree nut. They are high in heart-healthy unsaturated fat and many important nutrients such as calcium, zinc, and vitamins A, B, and E. Pecans also contain the highest amount of disease-fighting antioxidants as compared to all other tree nuts, so try to include these crunchy treats in your diet frequently in small amounts. However, you might want to save this dish for a very special evening—it is rich and scrumptious because of the high fat content of the nut breading.

1. Preheat the oven to 375°F. Line a baking pan with foil.

2. In a small shallow bowl, stir together the egg white and 1 teaspoon water. In another small shallow bowl, stir together the pecans, Parmesan, salt, and pepper.

3. Dip the pork chops in the egg mixture, letting the excess run off; then dredge in the pecan mixture. Place the pork chops on the prepared baking pan and cover with aluminum foil. Bake, covered, for 20 minutes. Remove the foil and bake for an additional 10 minutes, until browned.

TIP: *The breading mixture can also be made by pulsing the ingredients in a blender. You can use about 8 to 10 pecan halves in place of the finely chopped amount to get the right ratio.*

PAIR WITH . . . Broccoli with Lemon Butter (page 188)

1 egg white

¼ cup finely chopped pecans

2 tablespoons Parmesan cheese

Pinch sea salt

Pinch freshly ground black pepper

2 (4-ounce) pork loin chops, trimmed of fat

PER SERVING
Calories: 255
Fat: 12.5g
Saturated fat: 2.9g
Protein: 33.3g
Carbohydrates: 1.6g
Sodium: 218mg
Fiber: 1.5g
Sugar: 0.6g

Dijon Mustard Pork Tenderloin

A sweet mustard glaze brings out the taste of the pork, and the brown sugar ensures a golden caramelized crust on the finished tenderloin. This dish might become a summer favorite, so keep an eye on market tenderloin specials. You can mix up a big batch of marinade and store each tenderloin along with the appropriate amount of marinade in resealable bags in the freezer for up to 3 months. Simply thaw a tenderloin in the refrigerator overnight, still in the bag, and cook it the next day.

PREP TIME
10 MINUTES
(+ marinating time)

COOK TIME
20 MINUTES

1½ tablespoons Dijon mustard
1 tablespoon brown sugar
1 teaspoon balsamic vinegar
½ teaspoon minced garlic
½ teaspoon smoked paprika
1 (10-ounce) pork tenderloin, trimmed of fat

PER SERVING
Calories: 231
Fat: 5.5g
Saturated fat: 1.7g
Protein: 37.7g
Carbohydrates: 5.6g
Sodium: 216mg
Fiber: 0.6g
Sugar: 4.5g

1. In a medium bowl, stir together the mustard, brown sugar, vinegar, garlic, and paprika until well combined. Add the pork tenderloin to the bowl, turning it to coat. Cover the bowl with plastic wrap and refrigerate for at least 5 hours, and up to 10 hours.

2. Preheat the oven to 350°F.

3. Place the tenderloin in a baking dish, and add any marinade left in the bowl. Bake until the pork is no longer pink in the center, about 20 minutes. Let rest for 10 minutes before slicing.

TIP: *Tenderloin does not have to be cooked to be completely well done, because any threat of trichina, a parasite, is gone after 137°F. The USDA approves eating pork medium rare (internal temperature of 145°F), which is wonderful because pork can easily become dry if cooked too long.*

PAIR WITH . . . Mashed Roasted Butternut Squash (page 192)

Tomato Herb Flank Steak

PREP TIME
10 MINUTES
(+ marinating time)

COOK TIME
12 MINUTES

Tomato is a perfect marinade ingredient for this dish not only because it tastes divine when combined with beef but also, its acid tenderizes the meat. Flank steak is a tougher cut of beef, but it is very flavorful and worth the extra steps required to cook it well. Marinating and not overcooking this cut are an effective combination for creating a better texture. You should also always cut flank steak thinly against the grain in order to break up its long stringy muscle fibers.

1. Place the tomato, onion, garlic, red wine vinegar, and thyme in a blender, and pulse until smooth. Pour the tomato mixture into a resealable plastic bag and add the steak to the bag. Seal the bag and marinate the steak in the refrigerator overnight, turning at least once.

2. Preheat the grill to medium-high.

3. Grill the steak until it reaches your desired doneness, about 6 minutes per side for medium.

4. Transfer the cooked steak to a cutting board and let it stand for 10 minutes. Slice the steak thinly on the diagonal. Serve topped with the parsley.

TIP: *If you do not have access to a grill, this steak can be pan-seared in a large heavy-bottomed skillet over medium-high heat for about 5 minutes per side for medium.*

PAIR WITH . . . Bulgur Herb Pilaf (page 194)

1 tomato, coarsely chopped

½ red onion, coarsely chopped

1 clove garlic

3 tablespoons red wine vinegar

1 tablespoon chopped fresh thyme or 1 teaspoon dried thyme

¾ pound flank steak, trimmed of fat

1 tablespoon chopped fresh parsley or 1 teaspoon dried parsley

PER SERVING
Calories: 354
Fat: 14.3g
Saturated fat: 5.9g
Protein: 48.0g
Carbohydrates: 4.5g
Sodium: 99mg
Fiber: 1.3g
Sugar: 1.7g

Entertaining for Two

Asparagus Watercress Soup

If spring could be distilled down into one dish, it might look and taste like this pleasing green soup. Both main ingredients in this dish are delicate but have distinct flavors: The soup is earthy and bright tasting from the asparagus, with a peppery undertone from the watercress. The combination is a surprise in such a pale, elegant dish.

1. Melt the butter in a medium saucepan over medium heat. Sauté the scallion until softened, about 2 minutes. Stir in the flour until a paste forms and continue to cook until the paste is golden brown, about 3 minutes.

2. Pour in the chicken stock and bring the soup to a boil. Add the asparagus and watercress and reduce the heat to low. Cook, stirring, for about 5 minutes, or until the asparagus is tender.

3. Transfer the soup to a blender and pulse until very smooth. Add the yogurt and pulse until combined. Serve warm, not piping hot.

TIP: *If you are buying your watercress from a market, make sure that the herb has not flowered, because this will make the greens bitter and unpalatable. Watercress has more calcium than milk and is a better source of iron than spinach, so try to include it in salads, stews, and sandwiches every once in a while to provide some variety.*

PAIR WITH . . . Multigrain Chips (page 182)

1 tablespoon unsalted butter

1 scallion, white and green parts, chopped

1 tablespoon all-purpose flour

1 cup low-sodium chicken stock

10 asparagus spears, trimmed of woody ends and cut into 1-inch pieces

¾ cup stemmed, packed watercress

2 tablespoons fat-free plain Greek yogurt

PER SERVING

Calories: 110
Fat: 6.0g
Saturated fat: 3.7g
Protein: 6.1g
Carbohydrates: 8.8g
Sodium: 93mg
Fiber: 3.1g
Sugar: 2.9g

Roasted Baby Beets and Orange Salad

Beets are often not a first-choice salad ingredient, but they should be considered as such, because they are a rich source of dietary fiber, vitamin C, manganese, and iron. If you want a truly spectacular-looking salad, like a fiery sunset, try to source both red and yellow beets to add to the bright oranges of this dish. This salad isn't just divine looking; it is also a perfectly balanced blend of earthy beet and sweet-tart orange. Your taste buds will be in heaven. Note: See the instructions in Fresh Fruit Pasta Salad, page 128, for how to segment the orange while reserving its zest and juice.

PREP TIME
20 MINUTES

COOK TIME
35 MINUTES

4 baby beets, greens removed

1 navel orange, peeled and segmented

1 tablespoon balsamic vinegar

1 tablespoon olive oil

1 tablespoon freshly squeezed orange juice

1 teaspoon orange zest

½ teaspoon grainy mustard

Pinch sea salt

Pinch freshly ground black pepper

4 cups baby spinach or arugula

1 ounce goat cheese, crumbled

2 tablespoons chopped pecans

PER SERVING
Calories: 307
Fat: 17.7g
Saturated fat: 5.1g
Protein: 10.4g
Carbohydrates: 31.2g
Sodium: 347mg
Fiber: 9.0g
Sugar: 21.2g

1. Preheat the oven to 400°F.

2. Tear off a large piece of aluminum foil and place the beets in the center. Fold the foil to form a package and place it on a small baking sheet. Bake the beets until they are tender, about 35 minutes. Cool the beets, remove the skins, and cut them into eighths.

3. In a medium bowl, whisk together the balsamic vinegar, olive oil, orange juice and zest, and mustard. Season with salt and pepper. Add the spinach and toss to combine.

4. Arrange the dressed greens on two plates. Arrange the beets and oranges on the spinach. Top with goat cheese and pecans and serve.

TIP: *Beets can cause unsightly staining of everything they touch after you peel them, so take some care with your clothes. If your hands get stained, there are several techniques that can help you remove the color. You can rub your hands in fresh lemon juice until they are clean and rinse them thoroughly with water, or you can rub a fresh-cut potato on the stains if they aren't too extensive.*

PAIR WITH . . . Apple Cranberry Crumble (page 201)

PREP TIME
15 MINUTES

COOK TIME
60 MINUTES

Ratatouille

This is peasant stew full of ripe summer produce and herbs. Ratatouille is French in origin and part of its name, *touiller*, means "to stir or toss." This makes sense because the dish contains so many colorful ripe vegetables that are tossed together. Ratatouille is equally tasty either hot or cold and can be served alone or over rice or noodles for more substance. The variety of ingredients in this stew ensures a healthy wallop of nutrients, including vitamins A and C, calcium, iron, fiber, protein, and potassium. Ratatouille is also low in saturated fat and calories, making it the perfect dish for a healthy lifestyle.

Stir together all the ingredients except the salt and pepper in a large saucepan over medium-high heat. Bring to a boil, reduce the heat to low, and simmer until thick, about 1 hour. Season with salt and pepper.

TIP: *Try to cut the vegetables in this dish into uniform chunks so that they cook evenly when combined in the stew. You can either stew the ingredients until this dish is very tender and the flavors merge together or simmer them only until cooked so you can see the individual pieces of the vegetables. Both preparations are acceptable, and the taste will be the same.*

PAIR WITH . . . Fresh Gingered Melon (page 198)

½ small eggplant, peeled and diced into 1-inch chunks

1 zucchini, diced

1 red bell pepper, seeded, deribbed, and diced

1 red onion, diced

1 (15-ounce) can sodium-free diced tomato

⅓ cup low-sodium vegetable stock

1 teaspoon minced garlic

1 tablespoon fresh basil, or 1 teaspoon dried basil

½ teaspoon dried oregano

2 tablespoons chopped fresh parsley

Pinch red pepper flakes

Sea salt

Freshly ground black pepper

PER SERVING
Calories: 126
Fat: 0.7g
Saturated fat: 0.0g
Protein: 3.4g
Carbohydrates: 17.7g
Sodium: 53mg
Fiber: 7.3g
Sugar: 8.4g

Jambalaya

GLUTEN-FREE
DAIRY-FREE
MAKE AHEAD
ONE-POT

PREP TIME
15 MINUTES

COOK TIME
55 MINUTES

Freshly chopped vegetables, tender chicken, and juicy shrimp nestled in a spicy rice base create a dish that is both comforting and exotic. Jambalaya can have many other elements, including diced ham, sausage, and other seafood, so if you are feeling creative, try other ingredients in this dish. It is supposed to be made with relatively inexpensive ingredients or to use up what is in your refrigerator.

1 teaspoon olive oil

1 (5-ounce) skinless, boneless chicken breast, cut into strips

½ sweet onion, chopped

1 red bell pepper, seeded, deribbed, and diced

1 scallion, white and green parts, cut into ¼-inch-thick slices

1 teaspoon minced garlic

1 cup long-grain brown rice

2 large shrimp, peeled, deveined and coarsely chopped

1 cup sodium-free chicken stock

2 tablespoons Tabasco sauce

Pinch cayenne pepper

PER SERVING
Calories: 490
Fat: 7.8g
Saturated fat: 1.9g
Protein: 26.1g
Carbohydrates: 77.5g
Sodium: 192mg
Fiber: 4.7g
Sugar: 2.5g

1. Preheat the oven to 300°F.

2. Heat the olive oil in a large ovenproof skillet over medium-high heat. Sauté the chicken strips until just cooked, about 6 minutes. Remove the cooked chicken with a slotted spoon to a bowl. Set aside.

3. Add the onion, bell pepper, scallion, and garlic to the skillet, and sauté until the vegetables are softened, about 3 minutes. Return the cooked chicken to the skillet, and toss to combine. Add the rice, shrimp, stock, Tabasco, and cayenne. Bring to a boil; then reduce the heat to low. Simmer, stirring, for about 5 minutes.

4. Cover the skillet and put the jambalaya in the oven. Bake until the rice is tender and most of the liquid is absorbed, about 45 minutes.

TIP: *There are two different variations of jambalaya in Louisiana, where this dish originated: Cajun and Creole. This recipe is more Cajun in nature because it does not contain tomatoes and the meat is cooked separately from the onion and garlic.*

PAIR WITH . . . Citrus Curd with Berries (page 199)

PREP TIME
10 MINUTES

COOK TIME
55 MINUTES
(+ cooling time)

Lemon-Poached Salmon

Poached salmon is not as difficult as you might imagine, and the results are appealingly delicate. In this recipe, a light citrus, herbal taste complements the stronger-flavored salmon. If you are going to try this technique, it might be a good idea to double the recipe and have tender salmon fillets left over for salads and sandwiches. Salmon is a wonderful addition to a healthy diet because it is an excellent source of omega-3 fatty acids. This means salmon is heart friendly and can help improve brain health.

1. Put the water, lemon juice, onion, celery leaves, carrot, thyme, dill, bay leaf, pepper, and salt in a large saucepan over medium-high heat. Bring to a boil; then reduce the heat to low, and simmer for about 45 minutes. Remove from the heat and let cool for 15 minutes.

2. Strain the stock through a fine-mesh sieve into a large skillet, and discard the solids.

3. Place the skillet over low heat and bring the poaching liquid to a gentle simmer. Add the salmon fillets carefully and cover the skillet. Simmer until the fish looks opaque and is just cooked through, about 10 minutes.

4. Using a spatula, carefully transfer the fish to a plate and let cool completely before serving.

TIP: *Do not stir the poaching liquid at all while the salmon is in it or you may break the fillets. Also, make sure that the liquid does not boil, or your fish will end up overdone and tough.*

PAIR WITH . . . Quinoa Primavera (page 193)

4 cups water or low-sodium vegetable stock

¼ cup lemon juice

1 sweet onion, sliced

½ cup chopped celery leaves

½ cup sliced carrots

1 tablespoon fresh chopped thyme, or 1 teaspoon dried thyme

1 tablespoon fresh chopped dill, or 1 teaspoon dried dill

1 bay leaf

½ teaspoon freshly ground black pepper

Pinch sea salt

2 (6-ounce) skinless salmon fillets

PER SERVING

Calories: 338
Fat: 15.8g
Saturated fat: 2.2g
Protein: 49.5g
Carbohydrates: 0.0g
Sodium: 113mg
Fiber: 0.0g
Sugar: 0.0g

Spicy Calamari

Squid is a delectable low-fat and low-calorie source of protein, and high in vitamins B_2, B_3, and B_{12}. It is also a wonderful source of selenium, copper, and zinc. Eating calamari can boost your immune system, promote bone health, and reduce the risk of cardiovascular disease. The best way to cook this spicy recipe is on a grill, but you can also broil the squid if a grill is unavailable. Either technique produces a healthy dish, although the grill also adds a smoky undertone that is exceptional.

PREP TIME
15 MINUTES
(not including marinating time)

COOK TIME
6 MINUTES

1 teaspoon five-spice powder
½ teaspoon chili powder
¼ teaspoon ground cumin
¼ teaspoon ground coriander
1 teaspoon olive oil
3 large squid, cleaned and split open with tentacles cut into short lengths
Freshly ground black pepper
½ cup chopped cilantro
1 teaspoon lime zest

1. Mix the five-spice powder, chili powder, cumin, coriander, and olive oil in a medium bowl until a uniform paste forms. Add the squid and use your hands to rub the spice paste all over to coat. Cover the bowl with plastic wrap and marinate the squid in the refrigerator for at least 2 hours.

2. Preheat the grill to medium-high.

3. Grill the squid until just cooked, about 6 minutes. Season with pepper. Remove from the barbeque and serve topped with the cilantro and lime zest.

TIP: *Five-spice powder is a common spice mix used in Asian and Arabic cuisines. The most common blends can include anise, cinnamon, fennel seed, cloves, nutmeg, ginger, and turmeric.*

PAIR WITH . . . Broiled Tomatoes (page 192)

PER SERVING
Calories: 142
Fat: 4.3g
Saturated fat: 0.8g
Protein: 20.1g
Carbohydrates: 4.8g
Sodium: 65mg
Fiber: 0.0g
Sugar: 0.0g

Baked Salmon with Ruby Red Grapefruit Salsa

PREP TIME
10 MINUTES

COOK TIME
25 MINUTES

Citrus and fish is a natural pairing, which is why you often see lemon wedges served with seafood in restaurants. Lemon can serve different purposes depending on the fish and preparation method. Sometimes the lemon is meant to brighten and clarify the delicate flavor of the fish, and other times it can obscure a "fishy" taste found in some species. In this recipe tart, rosy grapefruit replaces the common lemon wedges and brightens the sweet, earthy flavor of the salmon.

1. Combine the grapefruit, bell pepper, scallion, jalapeño, honey, and thyme in a small bowl. Cover the salsa with plastic wrap and set aside in the refrigerator.

2. Preheat the oven to 400°F.

3. Lay two 2-foot-square pieces of aluminum foil on the work surface and fold them in half. Place the salmon fillets in the center of the foil pieces and sprinkle half of the lemon juice on each piece. Season with salt and pepper. Fold the foil to create sealed packets and place them on a baking sheet.

4. Bake the salmon until it is cooked through, about 25 minutes. Serve with the chilled salsa.

TIP: *Picking perfect grapefruit can be tricky, but even extra-tart fruit can work well with this salsa, so there is no waste. The fruit should be heavy for its size without overly thick skin. If your grapefruit does not have a strong fragrance, this does not mean it is not ripe; even ripe grapefruits only have a subtle scent at room temperature and none when cold.*

PAIR WITH . . . Herbed Egg Noodles (page 192)

1 ruby red grapefruit, peeled, sectioned, and chopped

½ red bell pepper, seeded, deribbed, and finely chopped

1 scallion, white and green parts, cut into ⅛-inch-thick slices

½ teaspoon minced fresh jalapeño pepper

1 tablespoon honey

1 tablespoon chopped fresh thyme, or 1 teaspoon dried thyme

2 (5-ounce) skinless salmon fillets

Juice of ½ lemon

Sea salt

Freshly ground black pepper

PER SERVING
Calories: 259
Fat: 9.0g
Saturated fat: 1.3g
Protein: 28.5g
Carbohydrates: 17.9g
Sodium: 183mg
Fiber: 2.0g
Sugar: 14.3g

Chicken-and-Melon-Stuffed Shells

MAKE AHEAD
30 MINUTES
ONE-POT

PREP TIME
25 MINUTES

If you want to impress your partner or special guests, then these delicate pastel-hued shells are a perfect appetizer or pasta course. Sweet ripe cantaloupe is a delightful contrast in what would be a savory dish without the melon. Cantaloupe is a very rich source of vitamins C and A as well as beta-carotene. It is important to thoroughly scrub the rind of cantaloupe before cutting into it in order to avoid any bacterial contamination. This dish is served chilled, and can be made in advance. Keep it in the refrigerator until you want to garnish and present it.

½ cup chopped
   cooked chicken

½ cup diced cantaloupe

½ cup diced English cucumber

½ red bell pepper, seeded,
   deribbed, and finely diced

2 tablespoons fat-free plain
   Greek yogurt

1 tablespoon freshly squeezed
   lime juice

1 tablespoon chopped fresh
   thyme, or 1 teaspoon
   dried thyme

Pinch sea salt

Pinch freshly ground
   black pepper

6 cooked jumbo
   manicotti shells

1. In a medium bowl mix together the chicken, cantaloupe, cucumber, bell pepper, yogurt, lime juice, thyme, salt, and pepper.

2. Spoon the filling into the manicotti shells and serve 3 per person.

TIP: *Save the cantaloupe seeds after removing them from the melon and rinse them very well in cold water. Pat them dry and bake the seeds in a very low-heat oven, about 160°F, for about 20 minutes or until crunchy. Cantaloupe seeds are a great source of healthy omega-3 fatty acids.*

PAIR WITH . . . Velvety Chocolate Pudding (page 202)

PER SERVING
Calories: 314
Fat: 3.4g
Saturated fat: 0.0g
Protein: 21.7g
Carbohydrates: 48.9g
Sodium: 159mg
Fiber: 1.3g
Sugar: 4.3g

PREP TIME
20 MINUTES

COOK TIME
15 MINUTES

Chicken Fajitas

Fajitas are festive wraps that are put together at the table and eaten with your hands. The meat is cut into thin strips to fit better in a tortilla and either pan-seared quickly or grilled to perfection. The toppings of this spicy dish vary depending on your preference, but you will often find rice, sautéed bell peppers and onions, salsa, sour cream, and shredded lettuce. This is a charming menu choice for entertaining a group because it can be doubled easily, and everything can be arranged in the middle of the table for an intimate meal.

1. Heat the olive oil in a large skillet over medium-high heat. Sauté the garlic until fragrant, about 1 minute. Add the chicken strips and sauté until cooked through but still juicy, about 6 minutes. Remove the chicken with a slotted spoon to a plate.

2. Add the bell peppers and onion to the skillet and sauté until softened, about 5 minutes. Stir in the chili powder, cumin, coriander, chicken strips and accumulated juices from the plate and sauté for 2 minutes.

3. Spoon the chicken filling onto the tortillas and top with the shredded lettuce and tomatoes. Roll up and serve 2 per person.

TIP: *If you want a gluten-free version of this dish, try using corn tortillas instead of whole-wheat. Always check the packaging very carefully on corn tortillas because some products are prepared in the same equipment with gluten-containing products, creating cross-contamination issues. Look for a gluten-free label on the tortillas.*

PAIR WITH . . . Citrus Curd with Berries (page 199)

½ teaspoon olive oil

1 teaspoon minced garlic

2 (6-ounce) boneless, skinless chicken breasts, cut into strips

1 red bell pepper, seeded, deribbed, and cut into ¼-inch-thick strips

1 green bell pepper, seeded, deribbed, and cut into strips

1 red onion, thinly sliced

1 teaspoon chili powder

½ teaspoon ground cumin

½ teaspoon ground coriander

4 (6-inch) whole-wheat tortillas, at room temperature

1 cup shredded lettuce

½ cup diced tomatoes

PER SERVING
Calories: 369
Fat: 8.1g
Saturated fat: 0.0g
Protein: 57.2g
Carbohydrates: 16.0g
Sodium: 220mg
Fiber: 5.0g
Sugar: 9.0g

Beef Stew

GLUTEN-FREE
DAIRY-FREE
MAKE AHEAD
ONE-POT

PREP TIME
20 MINUTES

COOK TIME
60 MINUTES

Versions of beef stew are found in most cuisines around the world, and this recipe is closely related to the traditional French preparation. When considering the cut of beef to use in your stew, stay away from the better cuts, such as sirloin, because time spent in a pot, simmering, will turn tender, fat-marbled beef tough. Lean cuts of beef are best because they have a great deal of collagen, a tough connective tissue that breaks down during long cooking, creating fork-tender chunks. Save your splurging for a full-bodied red wine to enjoy over a bowl of this flavorful stew.

1 teaspoon olive oil

6 ounces lean stewing beef, cut into ½-inch pieces

½ onion, chopped

½ cup halved button mushrooms

½ teaspoon minced garlic

1 cup canned low-sodium diced tomatoes

1 potato, peeled and diced into ½-inch chunks

1 carrot, peeled and sliced

1 cup low-sodium beef stock

¼ cup water

½ cup green beans, cut into 1-inch pieces

1 cup shredded fresh spinach

Freshly ground black pepper

1. Heat the olive oil in a large saucepan over medium-high heat. Brown the beef, about 5 minutes, and transfer to a plate with a slotted spoon. Set aside.

2. Add the onion, mushrooms, and garlic to the saucepan and sauté until softened, about 3 minutes. Return the beef to the pan and stir in the tomatoes, potatoes, carrot, stock, and water. Bring to a boil and reduce the heat to low. Simmer the stew, stirring occasionally, until the beef is tender, about 45 minutes.

3. Stir in the green beans and spinach. Simmer 2 more minutes and then remove from the heat. Season with pepper.

TIP: *You can substitute red wine for the water in this recipe to create a richer sauce. Try a merlot or robust cabernet sauvignon for the best results.*

PAIR WITH . . . Chocolate Oat Bites (page 201)

PER SERVING
Calories: 312
Fat: 7.9g
Saturated fat: 2.4g
Protein: 30.8g
Carbohydrates: 26.0g
Sodium: 175mg
Fiber: 4.9g
Sugar: 3.5g

PAIR WITH . . . RECIPES

A healthy lifestyle doesn't mean depriving yourself, and every good meal deserves a good accompaniment. In the pages that follow, you'll find delicious snacks, sides, and desserts that perfectly complement recipes for healthy living.

Many of the choices appear elsewhere in this book as suggested pairings. These accoutrements to the main entrées are also a great excuse for spending time with your special someone in the kitchen. Your partner can whip up smoothies while you tend to a stir-fry, or you can make chocolate pudding together while waiting for your baked pasta to come out of the oven. Make it fun.

These easy recipes are also great for parties. Simply double the amounts and serve your favorites buffet-style. Mix and match dips and chips at your next potluck. Make a few different desserts for a bake sale. Or have a private tasting party with your partner to decide which recipes you love the most.

Remember, this cookbook is a guide, not gospel. Use the lessons and meal-planning techniques from earlier in the book to suit your particular tastes and health goals. The possibilities, as they say, are endless, and experimenting with food pairings is both entertaining and satisfying, as well as a great way to expand your palate and spend time with your partner.

chapter 13

Pair with . . . Snacks

Peanut Butter Banana Smoothie

Place 1 peeled banana, ½ cup fat-free vanilla yogurt, ½ cup skim milk, 1 tablespoon peanut butter, and 1 tablespoon honey in a blender. Pulse until smooth.

PER SERVING (Calories 189, Fat: 4.0g, Saturated fat: 0.9g, Protein: 6.4g, Carbohydrates: 33.7g, Sodium: 97mg, Fiber: 2.5g, Sugar: 26.1g)

Many Berry Smoothie

Place 1 cup frozen strawberries, 1 cup frozen blueberries, 1 cup unsweetened apple juice, and ½ cup fat-free plain Greek yogurt in a blender. Pulse until very smooth and creamy.

PER SERVING (Calories: 152, Fat: 0.5g, Saturated fat: 0.0g, Protein: 4.4g, Carbohydrates: 34.2g, Sodium: 39mg, Fiber: 3.4g, Sugar: 27.8g)

Mango and Honey Smoothie

Peel, pit, and cut 1 mango into chunks. Place the chunks, 1 cup skim milk, ½ cup fat-free vanilla yogurt, 1 teaspoon honey, and 4 ice cubes in a blender. Pulse until smooth.

PER SERVING (Calories: 168, Fat: 0.3g, Saturated fat: 0.0g, Protein: 6.5g, Carbohydrates: 34.5g, Sodium: 102mg, Fiber: 1.9g, Sugar: 30.9g)

Multigrain Chips

Preheat the oven to 400°F and lightly coat a baking sheet with nonstick cooking spray. Cut 2 multigrain tortillas into 16 triangles each and spread them on the baking sheet without too much overlap. Sprinkle them with sea salt and freshly ground black pepper. Bake until crisp, turning once, about 5 minutes. Remove from the oven and cool on a wire rack. Store cooled chips in a sealed container.

PER SERVING (Calories: 140, Fat: 4.0g, Saturated fat: 1.0g, Protein: 5.0g, Carbohydrates: 23.0g, Sodium: 460mg, Fiber: 5.0g, Sugar: 2.0g)

Cinnamon Sugar Tortilla Chips with Berry Mint Salsa

Preheat the oven to 350°F. In a small bowl combine 1 teaspoon sugar with ¼ teaspoon ground cinnamon and set aside. Lay 2 whole-wheat tortillas on a cutting board and spray them with nonstick cooking spray. Sprinkle the tortillas with the cinnamon sugar and cut them into 16 triangles each. Spread triangles on 2 baking sheets and bake until crisp, about 10 minutes. Cool the chips on wire racks. In a medium bowl combine 1 cup quartered strawberries, ½ cup diced cucumber, 1 teaspoon chopped fresh cilantro, ½ teaspoon minced jalapeño pepper, and juice of ½ lime. Serve the berry salsa with the cinnamon chips.

PER SERVING (Calories: 145, Fat: 1.3g, Saturated fat: 0.0g, Protein: 4.7g, Carbohydrates: 30.8g, Sodium: 131mg, Fiber: 8.9g, Sugar: 5.5g)

Garlic and Herb Yogurt Dip

In a medium bowl thoroughly combine 1 cup fat-free plain Greek yogurt, 1 teaspoon lemon juice, ½ teaspoon minced garlic, ½ teaspoon dried dill, ¼ teaspoon dried basil, pinch sea salt, and pinch freshly ground black pepper. Serve with baked chips or cut-up vegetables.

PER SERVING (Calories: 56, Fat: 0.2g, Saturated fat: 0.0g, Protein: 7.7g, Carbohydrates: 5.7g, Sodium: 71mg, Fiber: 0.0g, Sugar: 5.4g)

Roasted Red Pepper Dip

Preheat the oven to broil and place 3 red bell peppers on a baking sheet. Broil the peppers until the skins are blackened, turning several times, about 5 minutes. Transfer the peppers to a small metal bowl and cover it tightly with plastic wrap. Let stand for about 15 minutes; then remove the skins and seeds from the peppers. Place the peppers, 2 teaspoons dried basil, 1 teaspoon minced garlic, 1 teaspoon olive oil, pinch sea salt, and pinch freshly ground black pepper in a blender and pulse until puréed but not completely smooth. Transfer to a bowl and serve with baked chips.

PER SERVING (Calories: 78, Fat: 2.9g, Saturated fat: 0.0g, Protein: 1.9g, Carbohydrates: 11.2g, Sodium: 124mg, Fiber: 3.8g, Sugar: 7.5g)

Spicy Maple Popcorn

Preheat the oven to 300°F and lightly coat a baking sheet with nonstick cooking spray. Lightly coat a medium bowl with cooking spray and put 3 cups plain popped popcorn in the bowl. In a small saucepan over medium heat, stir together 3 tablespoons maple syrup, 1 teaspoon butter, a pinch of sea salt, and a pinch of chili powder. Bring to a boil and boil for 2 minutes without stirring. Remove the pan from the heat and pour the syrup mixture over the popcorn. Stir to coat, spread the popcorn on the baking sheet, and bake for 15 minutes. Let the popcorn cool completely on the sheet; then break it up and store in a sealed container.

PER SERVING (Calories: 206, Fat: 3.5g, Saturated fat: 1.2g, Protein: 4.0g, Carbohydrates: 43.2g, Sodium: 135mg, Fiber: 5.0g, Sugar: 17.9g)

Coconut Energy Balls

Place ½ cup rolled oats, 2 dried figs, 3 tablespoons honey, 2 tablespoons chopped pecans, 2 tablespoons almond milk, 1 teaspoon sesame seeds, and a pinch of ground cinnamon in a food processor and pulse until the mixture holds together. Place ½ cup shredded unsweetened coconut on a plate. Form the oat mixture into 1-inch balls; then roll the balls in the coconut. Store coconut balls in a sealed container in the refrigerator.

PER SERVING (Calories: 264, Fat: 5.8g, Saturated fat: 3.5g, Protein: 4.0g, Carbohydrates: 53.1g, Sodium: 7mg, Fiber: 4.5g, Sugar: 35.7g)

Peanut Butter and Banana Tortilla Spirals

In a small bowl, stir together 2 tablespoons peanut butter and 2 tablespoons fat-free vanilla yogurt. Divide the peanut butter mixture evenly between two (8-inch) whole-wheat tortillas, spreading it out to the edges. Cut a ripe banana into thin slices and spread the banana on the tortillas. Sprinkle the bananas with a pinch ground cinnamon. Roll the tortillas up as tightly as possible and slice each tortilla into 4 pieces. Serve 4 pieces per person.

PER SERVING (Calories: 204, Fat: 9.0g, Saturated fat: 1.7g, Protein: 8.0g, Carbohydrates: Sodium: 203mg, Fiber: 4.0g, Sugar: 1.5g)

Pair with . . . Sides

Grilled Asparagus

Trim the woody ends off 16 asparagus spears and toss them with 1 teaspoon olive oil. Preheat a grill to medium-high or the oven to broil. Cook the asparagus on the grill or under a broiler until tender, about 3 minutes. Season with freshly ground black pepper.

PER SERVING (Calories: 46, Fat: 2.5g, Saturated fat: 0.0g, Protein: 2.8g, Carbohydrates: 5.0g, Sodium: 3mg, Fiber: 2.7g, Sugar: 2.4g)

Broccoli with Lemon Butter

Cut 1 head broccoli into florets and blanch them in boiling water until crisp-tender, about 3 minutes. Drain and transfer to a small bowl. Toss the hot broccoli with 1 teaspoon butter, 1 teaspoon freshly squeezed lemon juice, and ½ teaspoon lemon zest. Serve immediately.

PER SERVING (Calories: 48, Fat: 2.2g, Saturated fat: 1.2g, Protein: 2.6g, Carbohydrates: 5.9g, Sodium: 43mg, Fiber: 2.4g, Sugar: 1.5g)

North African-Spiced Carrots

Peel and very thinly slice 2 medium carrots; set aside. Heat 1 teaspoon olive oil in a medium saucepan over medium-high heat. When the oil is hot, add ½ teaspoon minced garlic, ½ teaspoon ground coriander, ½ teaspoon ground cumin, and ½ teaspoon paprika. Stir the spices for about 30 seconds; then add the carrots, ⅓ cup water, and 1 tablespoon freshly squeezed lemon juice. Bring to a boil; then reduce the heat and simmer until the carrots are tender and the liquid is almost absorbed, about 6 minutes. Stir in 1 tablespoon chopped fresh parsley.

PER SERVING (Calories: 51, Fat: 2.7g, Saturated fat: 0.0g, Protein: 0.8g, Carbohydrates: 6.8g, Sodium: 45mg, Fiber: 2.0g, Sugar: 3.1g)

Honey-and-Herb-Glazed Carrots

Peel ½ pound carrots and cut crosswise into ¼-inch slices. Blanch the carrots in boiling water until crisp-tender, about 4 minutes. Drain and transfer to a bowl. Toss the hot carrots with 1 teaspoon butter, 1 teaspoon honey, and 1 teaspoon chopped fresh thyme. Serve immediately.

PER SERVING (Calories: 73, Fat: 2.1g, Saturated fat: 1.2g, Protein: 1.1g, Carbohydrates: 13.6g, Sodium: 91mg, Fiber: 3.2g, Sugar: 8.0g)

Roasted Cauliflower

Preheat the oven to 450°F and lightly coat an 8-by-8-inch baking dish with non-stick cooking spray. Cut ½ head cauliflower into florets and in a small bowl toss the florets with 1 teaspoon olive oil and 2 teaspoons minced garlic. Transfer the cauliflower to the baking dish and bake for 10 minutes. Sprinkle the cauliflower with 2 tablespoons Parmesan cheese and bake for an additional 10 minutes, or until the cauliflower is tender.

PER SERVING (Calories: 133, Fat: 8.4g, Saturated fat: 4.3g, Protein: 11.0g, Carbohydrates: 5.8g, Sodium: 280mg, Fiber: 1.7g, Sugar: 1.6g)

Creamy Mashed Cauliflower

Cut ½ head cauliflower into florets and boil them until they are tender, about 10 minutes. Drain and purée the cauliflower with 1 teaspoon minced garlic and 3 tablespoons skim milk in a food processor until very creamy. Season with sea salt and freshly ground black pepper.

PER SERVING (Calories: 38, Fat: 0.1g, Saturated fat: 0.0g, Protein: 2.2g, Carbohydrates: 5.1g, Sodium: 110mg, Fiber: 1.7g, Sugar: 2.7g)

Wilted Greens

Melt 1 tablespoon butter in a large skillet over medium-high heat. Sauté 1 teaspoon minced garlic for 1 minute. Add 3 cups spinach or beet greens, 1 tablespoon freshly squeezed lemon juice, and 1 tablespoon water. Sauté the greens until they are wilted, about 3 minutes.

PER SERVING (Calories: 65, Fat: 6.0g, Saturated fat: 3.7g, Protein: 1.5g, Carbohydrates: 2.2g, Sodium: 78mg, Fiber: 1.1g, Sugar: 0.0g)

Sesame Green Beans

Preheat the oven to 400°F. Blanch 1 pound trimmed green beans in boiling water for about 2 minutes. Drain and transfer beans to a bowl. Add 1 tablespoon sesame seeds, 1 teaspoon sesame oil, and a pinch of red pepper flakes; toss to combine. Transfer the beans to a baking sheet and roast for 10 minutes. Season with sea salt.

PER SERVING (Calories: 116, Fat: 4.8g, Saturated fat: 0.7g, Protein: 4.9g, Carbohydrates: 17.2g, Sodium: 131mg, Fiber: 8.2g, Sugar: 3.2g)

Green Beans with Pecans

Wash and trim 1 pound green beans and blanch them in boiling water for 2 minutes. Drain and toss with 1 teaspoon butter, 2 tablespoons chopped pecans, 2 tablespoons dried cranberries, and freshly ground black pepper.

PER SERVING (Calories: 187, Fat: 12.1g, Saturated fat: 2.2g, Protein: 5.7g, Carbohydrates: 18.9g, Sodium: 27mg, Fiber: 9.5g, Sugar: 3.9g)

Sautéed Lemon Pepper Mushrooms

Melt 1 teaspoon butter in a large skillet over medium-high heat and add 1½ cups sliced button mushrooms. Sprinkle 1 teaspoon lemon zest on the mushrooms and let them cook undisturbed for 3 minutes. Stir the mushrooms and season with freshly ground black pepper. Sauté for an additional 5 minutes, until lightly browned. Serve topped with 1 teaspoon chopped fresh thyme.

PER SERVING (Calories: 29, Fat: 2.1g, Saturated fat: 1.2g, Protein: 1.7g, Carbohydrates: 1.9g, Sodium: 17mg, Fiber: 0.6g, Sugar: 1.0g)

Sautéed Mixed Vegetables

Cut 1 stalk broccoli into florets, peel 1 carrot and cut into ½-inch disks, and cut 1 red bell pepper into strips, cutting out and discarding the seeds and ribs. Blanch the vegetables in boiling water for about 3 minutes until crisp-tender. Drain and toss the vegetables with 1 teaspoon butter. Season with freshly ground black pepper.

PER SERVING (Calories: 52, Fat: 2.1g, Saturated fat: 1.2g, Protein: 1.6g, Carbohydrates: 7.3g, Sodium: 184mg, Fiber: 2.0g, Sugar: 3.7g)

Spring Vegetable Ragù

Heat 1 teaspoon olive oil in a medium saucepan over medium heat. Sauté 1 sliced scallion, 1 cup sliced zucchini, and ½ cup halved, trimmed snow peas until tender, about 3 minutes. Add 1 cup halved cherry tomatoes and ¼ cup water or vegetable stock. Bring to a simmer and cook, stirring often, until the tomatoes soften, about 2 minutes. Add 1 teaspoon chopped fresh basil and a pinch of red pepper flakes. Remove the pan from the heat and stir in ¼ cup Parmesan cheese. Serve plain or over pasta.

PER SERVING (Calories: 102, Fat: 5.4g, Saturated fat: 2.3g, Protein: 6.3g, Carbohydrates: 7.2g, Sodium: 142mg, Fiber: 1.8g, Sugar: 6.3g)

Simple Roasted New Potatoes

Preheat the oven to 400°F. Boil ½ pound new potatoes until tender, about 5 minutes. Remove from the heat and drain. Transfer the potatoes to a medium bowl and toss them with 1 teaspoon olive oil, 1 teaspoon minced garlic, ½ teaspoon chopped fresh thyme, ¼ teaspoon freshly ground black pepper, and a pinch of paprika. Spread potatoes on a baking sheet and roast until golden brown, about 15 minutes.

PER SERVING (Calories: 100, Fat: 2.4g, Saturated fat: 0.0g, Protein: 2.0g, Carbohydrates: 18.3g, Sodium: 7mg, Fiber: 2.8g, Sugar: 1.3g)

Roasted Root Vegetables

Preheat the oven to 350°F. Peel 1 sweet potato, 2 parsnips, and 2 carrots, and cut them into 1-inch chunks. In a medium bowl toss the vegetables with 1 teaspoon olive oil, 1 teaspoon brown sugar, and ½ teaspoon ground cinnamon. Transfer to a baking sheet and roast until tender and lightly caramelized, about 30 minutes. Season with freshly ground black pepper.

PER SERVING (Calories: 197, Fat: 3.0g, Saturated fat: 0.0g, Protein: 3.3g, Carbohydrates: 42.1g, Sodium: 76mg, Fiber: 10.4g, Sugar: 13.0g)

Sweet Potato Parsnip Mash

Peel 1 large sweet potato and 2 parsnips, and cut them into 1-inch chunks. Put the vegetables in a medium saucepan and cover them with water by 1 inch. Bring to a boil over medium-high heat and then reduce the heat to low. Simmer the vegetables until tender, about 20 minutes. Drain and mash with 1 tablespoon butter, ¼ teaspoon ground nutmeg, a pinch of sea salt, and a pinch of freshly ground black pepper using a potato masher. Do not mash until smooth; vegetables should still be a bit chunky.

PER SERVING (Calories: 133, Fat: 6.0g, Saturated fat: 3.7g, Protein: 1.9g, Carbohydrates: 18.8g, Sodium: 190mg, Fiber: 3.0g, Sugar: 5.9g)

Mashed Roasted Butternut Squash

Preheat the oven to 350°F. Peel and seed a small (about 1½ pounds) butternut squash and cut into 1-inch chunks. Toss the squash with 1 teaspoon olive oil and transfer to a baking sheet. Bake until the squash is tender, about 30 minutes. Transfer to a bowl and mash with 1 teaspoon of butter, using a potato masher. Season with sea salt and freshly ground black pepper.

PER SERVING (Calories: 131, Fat: 4.5g, Saturated fat: 1.6g, Protein: 2.1g, Carbohydrates: 24.6g, Sodium: 139mg, Fiber: 4.2g, Sugar: 4.6g)

Broiled Tomatoes

Preheat the oven to broil. Cut 1 large tomato in half, place the halves in a small baking dish, and drizzle the tops with 1 tablespoon olive oil. Sprinkle the tomatoes with ¼ teaspoon minced garlic. Broil tomatoes for about 5 minutes, until softened. Sprinkle with 1 teaspoon chopped fresh basil and freshly ground black pepper.

PER SERVING (Calories: 77, Fat: 7.2g, Saturated fat: 1.4g, Protein: 0.9g, Carbohydrates: 4.0g, Sodium: 4.5mg, Fiber: 1.2g, Sugar: 2.4g)

Parmesan-Sautéed Zucchini

Slice 3 medium zucchini into ½-inch rounds and set aside. Heat 1 teaspoon olive oil in a large skillet over medium-high heat. Sauté 1 teaspoon minced garlic until softened, about 2 minutes. Add the sliced zucchini and sauté until the squash is lightly browned, about 6 minutes. Add ¼ cup of Parmesan cheese and pinch freshly ground black pepper. Toss until the cheese melts, about 2 minutes.

PER SERVING (Calories: 114, Fat: 5.9g, Saturated fat: 2.4g, Protein: 8.2g, Carbohydrates: 10.8 g, Sodium: 160mg, Fiber: 3.3g, Sugar: 5.1g)

Herbed Egg Noodles

Cook ¼ pound egg noodles in boiling water until al dente, about 10 minutes. Drain and toss with 1 teaspoon butter, 1 teaspoon chopped fresh thyme, ½ teaspoon chopped fresh basil, and a pinch of freshly ground black pepper.

PER SERVING (Calories: 96, Fat: 3.1g, Saturated fat: 1.5g, Protein: 2.6g, Carbohydrates: 14.6g, Sodium: 17mg, Fiber: 0.9g, Sugar: 0.0g)

Quinoa Primavera

Rinse ½ cup quinoa well and put it in a small saucepan with 1 cup water. Bring to a boil over medium-high heat; then reduce the heat and simmer, covered, until the quinoa is tender and the water is absorbed, about 20 minutes. Remove the pan from the heat and set aside. Heat ½ teaspoon olive oil in a large skillet over medium-high heat. Sauté ½ teaspoon minced garlic; 1 small peeled, grated carrot; 1 small diced red bell pepper; ¼ cup diced celery; and 1 sliced scallion, white and green parts, until the vegetables are tender. Add the cooked quinoa and stir to combine. Season with sea salt and freshly ground black pepper.

PER SERVING (Calories: 190, Fat: 3.7g, Saturated fat: 0.0g, Protein: 6.7g, Carbohydrates: 32.7g, Sodium: 102mg, Fiber: 4.8g, Sugar: 4.2g)

Garlic Quinoa

Rinse ½ cup quinoa well and put it in a small saucepan with 1 cup water and ½ teaspoon minced garlic. Bring to a boil and then reduce heat and simmer, covered, until the quinoa is tender and the water is absorbed, about 20 minutes. Fluff quinoa with a fork and season with sea salt and freshly ground black pepper.

PER SERVING (Calories: 148, Fat: 2.4g, Saturated fat: 0.0g, Protein: 5.7g, Carbohydrates: 25.9g, Sodium: 2mg, Fiber: 2.8g, Sugar: 0.0g)

Cinnamon Couscous

Melt 1 teaspoon butter in a medium saucepan over medium-high heat. Sauté 1 sliced scallion, white and green parts, and ½ teaspoon ground cinnamon for 1 minute. Add ½ cup apple juice and ½ cup water to the saucepan. Bring to a boil and then remove from the heat. Stir in ½ cup couscous and cover the saucepan. Let stand for 5 minutes; then fluff couscous with a fork. Serve topped with 2 tablespoons slivered almonds.

PER SERVING (Calories: 212, Fat: 2.3g, Saturated fat: 1.3g, Protein: 5.7g, Carbohydrates: 41.8g, Sodium: 21mg, Fiber: 2.7g, Sugar: 6.9g)

Bulgur Herb Pilaf

Bring 1 cup bulgur and 1½ cups water to a boil in a medium saucepan. Reduce the heat and simmer for about 15 minutes, or until the bulgur is tender. Drain and fluff bulgur with a fork. Stir in 1 teaspoon butter, ½ teaspoon minced garlic, 1 sliced scallion, white and green parts, and 1 tablespoon chopped fresh cilantro. Season with sea salt and freshly ground black pepper.

PER SERVING (Calories: 262, Fat: 2.8g, Saturated fat: 1.4g, Protein: 8.7g, Carbohydrates: 54.4g, Sodium: 31mg, Fiber: 13.3g, Sugar: 0.8g)

Pistachio Rice Pilaf

Melt 1 teaspoon butter in a medium saucepan over medium-high heat. Sauté 1 teaspoon minced garlic and 1 sliced scallion, white and green parts, until tender, about 2 minutes. Add ½ cup rice and stir to coat. Add ¾ cup low-sodium chicken stock and bring to a boil. Reduce heat and cook, covered, until all the liquid is absorbed, about 20 minutes. Stir in 2 tablespoons chopped pistachios and 2 tablespoons dried cranberries. Serve warm or cold.

PER SERVING (Calories: 193, Fat: 5.4g, Saturated fat: 1.6g, Protein: 5.0g, Carbohydrates: 32.1g, Sodium: 47mg, Fiber: 1.7g, Sugar: 0.4g)

Banana Basmati Rice

Slice 1 ripe banana into ½-inch disks. Place a medium saucepan over medium-low heat and melt 1 teaspoon butter. Add the banana slices and sauté until the fruit caramelizes, about 3 minutes. Add 1 cup cooked basmati rice and stir gently until the rice is heated through. Season with a pinch of sea salt and serve.

PER SERVING (Calories: 169, Fat: 1.9g, Saturated fat: 1.2g, Protein: 2.6g, Carbohydrates: 36.9g, Sodium: 118mg, Fiber: 1.8g, Sugar: 7.0g)

Pair with . . . Desserts

Fresh Gingered Melon

Cut 1 small (2-pound) peeled and seeded cantaloupe into 1-inch chunks and toss with 2 tablespoons honey and ½ teaspoon ground ginger. Refrigerate for at least 30 minutes and serve topped with ½ teaspoon chopped fresh thyme.

PER SERVING (Calories: 140, Fat: 0.4g, Saturated fat: 0.0g, Protein: 2.0g, Carbohydrates: 35.6g, Sodium: 36mg, Fiber: 2.1g, Sugar: 34.6g)

Tropical Fruit Salad with Creamy Lime Sauce

Peel and core a small (2-pound) pineapple and cut it into 1-inch chunks. Toss the pineapple with 1 sliced banana. In a small bowl whisk together ½ cup fat-free vanilla Greek yogurt, 1 tablespoon honey, and 1 tablespoon freshly squeezed lime juice. Serve chopped fruit topped with creamy lime sauce and 1 tablespoon unsweetened shredded coconut per serving.

PER SERVING (Calories: 218, Fat: 1.0g, Saturated fat: 0.8g, Protein: 6.6g, Carbohydrates: 49.9g, Sodium: 24mg, Fiber: 4.5g, Sugar: 37.5g)

Mixed Berries with Orange Cream

In a small bowl stir together ¼ cup fat-free plain Greek yogurt, 1 tablespoon freshly squeezed orange juice, and ¼ teaspoon orange zest until well blended. Set aside. In a medium bowl toss together 1 cup hulled and halved strawberries, ½ cup raspberries, and ½ cup blueberries. Spoon the berries into two serving bowls and top evenly with the orange cream. Refrigerate the bowls before serving.

PER SERVING (Calories: 93, Fat: 0.6g, Saturated fat: 0.0g, Protein: 4.2g, Carbohydrates: 20.3g, Sodium: 54mg, Fiber: 9.5g, Sugar: 12.6g)

Speedy Strawberry Ice Cream

Place 3 cups frozen strawberries and 2 tablespoons sugar in a food processor and pulse until the berries are coarsely chopped. Keep the processor running and slowly pour in ¼ cup fat-free half-and-half until smooth and creamy. Serve immediately or freeze in a sealed container for up to one week.

PER SERVING (Calories: 169, Fat: 0.0g, Saturated fat: 0.0g, Protein: 0.0g, Carbohydrates: 34.5g, Sodium: 65mg, Fiber: 4.5g, Sugar: 27.4g)

Citrus Curd with Berries

Whisk together ⅓ cup sugar, ¼ cup freshly squeezed orange juice, 2 tablespoons freshly squeezed lemon juice, a pinch of sea salt, and 3 large egg yolks in a small saucepan. Place the saucepan over medium heat and cook, whisking constantly, until the curd is thick, about 6 to 8 minutes. Remove the curd from the heat and whisk in 2 teaspoons butter and 1 teaspoon lemon zest. Spoon the curd into a bowl and cover it with plastic wrap, pressing the wrap right onto the surface. Refrigerate and chill completely, about 2 hours. Fill two serving bowls with about 1 cup berries each, any type, and top with citrus curd.

PER SERVING (Calories: 303, Fat: 11.2g, Saturated fat: 5.0g, Protein: 5.4g, Carbohydrates: 48.9g, Sodium: 161mg, Fiber: 11.2g, Sugar: 43.4g)

Fruit Tarts

Preheat the oven to 375°F and lightly coat two (4-inch) tart pans with nonstick cooking spray. In a medium bowl stir together ½ cup all-purpose flour, ¼ cup oats, and 2 tablespoons brown sugar until well blended. Stir in 2 tablespoons skim milk and 1 tablespoon canola oil until the dough just holds together. Press the dough into the tart pans evenly and prick with a fork. Bake the tart shells until lightly browned, 13 to 15 minutes, and then cool the shells on a wire rack for about 10 minutes. Pop the tart shells out of the pans carefully and cool the shells completely on the racks. Spoon ¼ cup fat-free vanilla Greek yogurt into each shell and heap about ½ cup of mixed fresh fruit onto the yogurt. Refrigerate the tarts, covered, up to 2 hours, until you want to serve them.

PER SERVING (Calories: 279, Fat: 8.0g, Saturated fat: 0.7g, Protein: 5.6g, Carbohydrates: 47.4g, Sodium: 17mg, Fiber: 2.4g, Sugar: 14.2g)

Nutmeg-Baked Peaches

Preheat the oven to 350°F. Use a peeler to take the skin off two peaches and then halve them and remove the pits. Place the peach halves hollow-side-up in a small baking dish. In a small bowl combine 2 tablespoons chopped pecans, 1 tablespoon brown sugar, ½ teaspoon grated orange zest, and a pinch of nutmeg. Divide the nut mixture among all four peach halves. Bake the peaches in the oven until the fruit is soft, about 20 minutes. Serve two peach halves each warm from the oven.

PER SERVING (Calories: 105, Fat: 5.3g, Saturated fat: 0.6g, Protein: 1.7g, Carbohydrates: 15.0g, Sodium: 1mg, Fiber: 2.3g, Sugar: 12.9g)

Pecan Honey Bananas

Melt 1 tablespoon coconut oil in a large skillet over medium heat. Slice two bananas and arrange the slices in a single layer in the skillet. Cook the slices 1 minute per side for a total of 2 minutes. Arrange the slices on two plates and drizzle them with 1 tablespoon honey for each plate. Sprinkle a pinch of cinnamon on the bananas and top with 1 teaspoon of chopped pecans. Serve warm.

PER SERVING (Calories: 220, Fat: 9.3g, Saturated fat: 6.2g, Protein: 1.6g, Carbohydrates: 36.0g, Sodium: 2mg, Fiber: 3.9g, Sugar: 22.8g)

Ricotta Banana Split

In a small bowl stir together ½ cup fat-free ricotta cheese, 1 teaspoon sugar, and 1 teaspoon pure vanilla extract until smooth. Slice a ripe banana into 1-inch slices and divide them evenly between two serving bowls. Top the banana evenly with the cheese mixture and spoon 3 tablespoons canned crushed pineapple into each bowl. Top the pineapple with 1 tablespoon chopped dark chocolate and 1 teaspoon chopped pecans. Serve immediately.

PER SERVING (Calories: 156, Fat: 3.0g, Saturated fat: 0.5g, Protein: 6.1g, Carbohydrates: 23.8g, Sodium: 66mg, Fiber: 2.3g, Sugar: 13.7g)

Cheese-Stuffed Pears

Preheat the oven to broil. Cut 2 ripe pears in half and scoop out the cores. Place the pear halves in a small baking dish and broil until tender, about 10 minutes. In a small bowl stir together ¼ cup fat-free cottage cheese, 1 tablespoon honey, and ¼ teaspoon ground nutmeg. Spoon the cheese mixture into the hollows in the pears and serve warm.

PER SERVING (Calories: 177, Fat: 0.3g, Saturated fat: 0.0g, Protein: 4.6g, Carbohydrates: 42.9g, Sodium: 153mg, Fiber: 6.6g, Sugar: 30.7g)

Chunky Applesauce

Place 4 peeled, cored, and chopped apples, ½ cup water, and 2 tablespoons pure maple syrup in a medium saucepan over medium-low heat. Cook the apple mixture, stirring occasionally until the liquid simmers; then reduce the heat to low and simmer for about 15 minutes, until the fruit is tender. Remove from the heat and stir in 1 teaspoon ground cinnamon, ¼ teaspoon ground nutmeg, a pinch of ginger, and pinch cloves. Mash with a potato masher to create a chunky, thick applesauce. Transfer the applesauce to a container and allow to cool, or serve warm.

PER SERVING (Calories: 242, Fat: 0.0g, Saturated fat: 0.0g, Protein: 0.0g, Carbohydrates: 63.7g, Sodium: 5mg, Fiber: 8.8g, Sugar: 49.8g)

Apple Cranberry Crumble

Preheat the oven to 350°F and lightly coat two (8-ounce) ramekins with non-stick cooking spray and set aside. Peel, core, and dice 2 sweet apples and toss them together with ½ cup cranberries and 1 tablespoon granulated sugar in a small bowl. Divide the fruit mixture evenly between the ramekins. In a small bowl combine ¼ cup rolled oats, 2 tablespoons all-purpose flour, 1 tablespoon brown sugar, 1 tablespoon pecans, ¼ teaspoon ground cinnamon and a pinch of salt until well mixed. Mix in 1 tablespoon melted butter until the mixture resembles coarse crumbs. Sprinkle the crumble mixture over the fruit and bake until the fruit is tender and bubbly, about 30 minutes. Serve warm.

PER SERVING (Calories: 288, Fat: 9.0g, Saturated fat: 4.0g, Protein: 2.7g, Carbohydrates: 52.1g, Sodium: 45mg, Fiber: 7.3g, Sugar: 30.5g)

Chocolate Oat Bites

Put ¼ cup peanut butter, 2 tablespoons brown sugar, 1 tablespoon milk, 1 teaspoon pure vanilla extract, and 1 teaspoon cocoa powder in a medium saucepan over medium-high heat. Bring to a simmer, stirring, and remove from the heat. Stir in ½ cup rolled oats and 1 tablespoon sesame seeds until well mixed. Divide mixture into 6 cookies and place them on a parchment-lined plate. Refrigerate until firm, about 30 minutes, and serve.

PER SERVING (Calories: 329, Fat: 20.1g, Saturated fat: 4.1g, Protein: 12.0g, Carbohydrates: 31.2g, Sodium: 156mg, Fiber: 4.8g, Sugar: 12.6g)

Velvety Chocolate Pudding

Put 3 tablespoons sugar, 1 tablespoon cocoa powder, 1 tablespoon cornstarch, and a pinch of salt in a medium saucepan and whisk thoroughly. Whisk in 1 cup 2% milk and then place the saucepan over medium heat. Bring the mixture to a boil, whisking constantly, and then reduce the heat to low. Simmer until the pudding is thick, about 2 minutes, and remove the pan from the heat. Whisk in 1 ounce finely chopped dark chocolate and 1 teaspoon pure vanilla extract until very smooth. Spoon the pudding into serving dishes and cover them with plastic wrap, pressing it right onto the surface. Refrigerate ramekins in the refrigerator until chilled, about 3 hours.

PER SERVING (Calories: 232, Fat: 7.1g, Saturated fat: 4.7g, Protein: 5.6g, Carbohydrates: 37.8g, Sodium: 147mg, Fiber: 1.3g, Sugar: 31.1g)

Maple Pecan Tapioca Pudding

Stir together 1 cup skim milk, 1 egg, 2 tablespoons tapioca, and a pinch of salt in a medium saucepan and let stand for 10 minutes until the tapioca thickens a little. Place the pan over medium heat and bring to a boil, stirring constantly. Cook, stirring, until the pudding is very thick and the tapioca plumps up, about 10 to 15 minutes. Remove the pan from the heat and stir in ¼ cup pure maple syrup, 1 teaspoon pure vanilla extract, and ¼ teaspoon ground cinnamon. Spoon pudding into two serving dishes and refrigerate for at least 45 minutes. Serve topped with 1 teaspoon chopped pecans.

PER SERVING (Calories: 270, Fat: 7.3g, Saturated fat: 1.2g, Protein: 7.5g, Carbohydrates: 42.9g, Sodium: 177mg, Fiber: 1.0g, Sugar: 30.8g)

THE DIRTY DOZEN and the CLEAN 15

If you are committed to eating healthy food, then heaps of fruits and vegetables are a huge part of your meals. One of the questions that will crop up is whether to buy organic or not. Most commercially grown produce is contaminated to a certain degree with chemicals and pesticides that can have damaging effects on your health. So organic food is a logical choice if you have an eye on longevity and wellness.

Unfortunately, organic fruits and vegetables can be expensive and unavailable in some areas. This means you have to pick and choose which organic produce to buy. A nonprofit environmental watchdog organization called Environmental Working Group (EWG) makes this choice a little easier. The EWG looks at data supplied by the US Department of Agriculture and the US Food and Drug Administration regarding pesticide residues and compiles a list each year outlining the pesticide loads found in commercial crops. You can use these lists to decide which fruits or vegetables to buy organic (the "Dirty Dozen") in order to minimize your exposure to pesticides and which produce is considered safe enough to purchase conventionally grown (the "Clean 15"). These lists change every year, so make sure to look up the most recent before you fill your shopping cart.

The 2014 DIRTY DOZEN

➤ Apples
➤ Celery
➤ Cherry tomatoes
➤ Cucumbers
➤ Grapes
➤ Nectarines (imported)
➤ Peaches
➤ Potatoes
➤ Snap peas (imported)
➤ Spinach
➤ Strawberries
➤ Sweet bell peppers

Plus produce contaminated with highly toxic organophosphate insecticides:

➤ Blueberries (domestic)
➤ Hot peppers

There is also a list from the EWG that outlines foods that have the least pesticide contamination and can be purchased from commercially grown crops. This does not mean they are pesticide-free, so wash these fruits and vegetables thoroughly.

The CLEAN 15

➤ Asparagus
➤ Avocados
➤ Cabbage
➤ Cantaloupe (domestic)
➤ Cauliflower
➤ Eggplant
➤ Grapefruit
➤ Kiwi
➤ Mangos
➤ Onions
➤ Papayas
➤ Pineapples
➤ Sweet corn
➤ Sweet peas (frozen)
➤ Sweet potatoes

It is important to remember that the positive impact of eating a diet rich in fruits and vegetables far outweighs the risk of pesticide exposure.

MEASUREMENT CONVERSIONS

VOLUME EQUIVALENTS (LIQUID)

US STANDARD	US STANDARD (OUNCES)	METRIC (APPROXIMATE)
2 tablespoons	1 fl. oz.	30 mL
¼ cup	2 fl. oz.	60 mL
½ cup	4 fl. oz.	120 mL
1 cup	8 fl. oz.	240 mL
1½ cups	12 fl. oz.	355 mL
2 cups or 1 pint	16 fl. oz.	475 mL
4 cups or 1 quart	32 fl. oz.	1 L
1 gallon	128 fl. oz.	4 L

OVEN TEMPERATURES

FAHRENHEIT (F)	CELSIUS (C) (APPROXIMATE)
250	120
300	150
325	165
350	180
375	190
400	200
425	220
450	230

VOLUME EQUIVALENTS (DRY)

US STANDARD	METRIC (APPROXIMATE)
⅛ teaspoon	0.5 mL
¼ teaspoon	1 mL
½ teaspoon	2 mL
¾ teaspoon	4 mL
1 teaspoon	5 mL
1 tablespoon	15 mL
¼ cup	59 mL
⅓ cup	79 mL
½ cup	118 mL
⅔ cup	156 mL
¾ cup	177 mL
1 cup	235 mL
2 cups or 1 pint	475 mL
3 cups	700 mL
4 cups or 1 quart	1 L
½ gallon	2 L
1 gallon	4 L

WEIGHT EQUIVALENTS

US STANDARD	METRIC (APPROXIMATE)
½ ounce	15 g
1 ounce	30 g
2 ounces	60 g
4 ounces	115 g
8 ounces	225 g
12 ounces	340 g
16 ounces or 1 pound	455 g

RESOURCES

Environmental Working Group. "EWG's 2014 Shopper's Guide to Pesticides in Produce." Accessed May 10, 2014. http://www.ewg.org/foodnews/list.php.

Haas, Elson, and Buck Levin. *Staying Healthy with Nutrition, rev.: The Complete Guide to Diet and Nutritional Medicine*. Berkeley, CA: Celestial Arts, 2006.

University of Nebraska–Lincoln. "Food Storage Chart for Cupboard/Pantry, Refrigerator and Freezer." Accessed May 9, 2014. http://food.unl.edu/safety/chart.

US Department of Agriculture Food Safety and Inspection Service. "Leftovers and Food Safety." Accessed May 12, 2014. http://www.fsis.usda.gov/wps/portal/fsis/topics/food-safety-education/get-answers/food-safety-fact-sheets/safe-food-handling/leftovers-and-food-safety.

RECIPE INDEX

INDEX

CPSIA information can be obtained
at www.ICGtesting.com
Printed in the USA
LVHW02s1608101217
559210LV00001B/1/P